Lessons From A Gathering of Men

How Men's Work Is Redefining Masculinity
And Improving Men's Lives

© 2016 by Michael Taylor

Published by Creation Publishing Group LLC

1219 Nikki Lane ~ Stafford, Texas 77477

www.creationpublishing.com

ISBN 978-0-9969487-2-2

Library of Congress Control Number: 2016911379

All rights reserved. No part of this book may be reproduced, stored in a retrieval system or transmitted in any form or by any means without the prior written permission of the publishers, except by a reviewer who may quote brief passages in a review to be printed in a newspaper, magazine, journal or other digital media.

Table of Contents

Introduction 5

Acknowledgements 7

Foreword 9

Chapter 1 A Shift in Male Consciousness 13

Chapter 2 Men's Emotional Healing 23

Chapter 3 The Awakened Male 45

Chapter 4 What Is A Men's Group? 73

Chapter 5 What Are The Benefits Of Men's Work? 89

Chapter 6 Diversity 119

Chapter 7 What Men Are Saying About Men's Work 133

    Michael Over 136

    Boysen Hodgson 157

    Richard Arsic 172

    Tom Kelley 183

Enric Carbo 194

Graham Reid Phoenix 204

Brett Churnin 214

Chapter 8 Why Join A Men's Group? 225

Chapter 9 Starting A Men's Group 233

Chapter 10 Resources 245

Recommended Reading 251

About the Author 253

Introduction

For the past 20 years or so I've been writing about men's issues and attempting to engage men in a new conversation about masculinity. When I first began writing, there were very few resources available to men who were ready to engage in this type of dialog. At times I felt isolated and alone but there was a part of me that instinctively knew there were other men who were ready to redefine the roles of manhood.

As I fast forward to January 2017, a lot has changed. With the advent of the Internet and the fast pace of technology growth, I now see how my vision from long ago is beginning to manifest on a global scale. Because of the Internet, I have been able to positively engage men around the globe with my positive message of creating a new paradigm of masculinity for men.

In addition to my work, there are now thousands of coaches, therapists, authors, motivational speakers and organizations that are ushering in new ways for men to interact and relate in this ever-changing world we live in. In no way am I saying I'm responsible for this change. I'm simply acknowledging that my vision of redefining masculinity is being manifested in ways that I only dreamt of twenty years ago.

I am filled with a deep sense of optimism and hope for the future for all men. This optimism arises out of my belief in human evolution and transformation. I do not accept the media generated perception that the world is getting worse and we are headed down a path of destruction. Quite the contrary, I believe we are living in the most opportunistic times in the history of our planet and the future is filled with unlimited possibilities for anyone who is willing to put forth the effort. But most importantly, I'm excited about the evolution of masculinity which I believe will usher in a new way of being and relating on the planet that is going to begin eradicating the majority of social challenges facing our world.

This book is my attempt to share my optimism in hopes that more men and women will embrace a new paradigm of masculinity which I believe can transform the world.

Acknowledgements

First, foremost and always, I must acknowledge the Divine Intelligence that created and is still creating this amazing universe we live in. This Intelligence goes by many names but I simply refer to it as The Source. I acknowledge The Source for my gifts, passion and persistence in sharing my ideas with the world. I am grateful to have created a deep connection and intimacy with The Source and it is the driving force of my life. It infuses me with creativity, optimism, patience and a deep sense of purpose as I allow it to guide me to fulfill my life's purpose. So to The Source I simply say, THANK YOU for everything. My life is a miracle!

To: *Graham Reid Phoenix*, I would like to acknowledge you for your vision of a virtual men's group and accepting me into the group. I must admit that I was a bit skeptical at first about the effectiveness of an online virtual men's group. However, it has been a source of great growth and connection for me and I am so glad I joined.

To: *Tom Kelley, Richard Arsic, Boysen Hodgson. Enric Carbó, Eivind Figenschau Skjellum, Jeffrey Platts, Michael Over and Luis Louro Oliveira*. I want to thank each of you for how you show up in the Virtual Men's Gathering (VMG) Group. It has been an honor and a pleasure to engage with you on this journey and I feel deeply blessed to be able to call you my friends. I look forward to continued growth and success in all areas of our lives.

To: *Brett Churnin*, although you aren't a part of the VMG Group, your work with supporting men in creating men's groups is extremely important. The reason I put this book together is to provide men with a resource to support their growth, and your work definitely does that. You left an indelible mark with me at the Shift Networks Men's Conference and I'm glad we are still working together to bring men's work to the masses. Good luck!

To all the men who are ready to receive the message in this book, I simply say Welcome! This book is a labor of love that I hope will bring you insights and wisdom to support you in living a rewarding and fulfilling life. Since you are reading this book, I am going to assume that you are ready to take 100% responsibility for your life and my hope is that this book supports you in doing so. This book is written as a guide to support you in navigating this amazing gift called life and to help you embrace authentic masculinity that allows you to be and express who you really are without the confines and restraints of an antiquated masculine culture. It's time for you to wake up to who and what you really are and to become the amazing man I know you are capable of becoming.

Good luck!

Foreword

Michael Taylor has been a friend of mine for over six years, ever since we met at the 'Evolving Men's Conference' in Boulder, Colorado, in 2010. Both of us have been writing, broadcasting and coaching for men for longer than that. When we met, we found that, independently, we had re-created ourselves out of the disasters of our lives. We both found we had the desire to take what we had done and make it available for men everywhere.

One of the most important aspects of the work we do is developing the connections between men. This starts with our own connections with men. We achieve this partly through the men's groups that we belong to where the connection we find is the essential bedrock that we build the rest of our work on.

We are in a men's group together, even though we live on opposite sides of the Atlantic Ocean. We meet every other Friday for ninety minutes with other men from around the world. There are men from the United States, Canada, the United Kingdom, Norway, Spain, Portugal and the Czech Republic. We are of different ages, cultures, colors and races who share our lives and our problems as men.

I created this group, the 'Virtual Men's Gathering', three years ago because I live in remote rural Spain and I could find no men around me to meet with. So I harnessed the power of the Internet to set up a virtual meeting where we can sit in a circle and look each other in the eye, and be present with each other. Michael was one of the first men to join me in the group, along with many of the men who write about their experiences in this book.

In the book, I talk about the process I went through in my life that brought me to creating this group. What is crucial for you to know is that being in this group has transformed my life. All the men I know who are creating transformation in their lives are doing it through being in a men's group, either face to face or virtually. With modern technology, location is no longer a block to finding or creating a group. You can just step up and do it.

There is a lot in this book about the importance of the connection created by being in a circle with other like-minded men. I want to emphasize this now: connection is everything. It is the way to heal our souls and it is the way we grow and develop. As Johann Wolfgang von Goethe said,

> *"The world is so empty if one thinks only of mountains, rivers & cities; but to know someone who thinks & feels with us, & who, though distant, is close to us in spirit, this makes the earth for us an inhabited garden."*

I want to finish by quoting Michael as he talks about men and men's work,

> *"Real men understand that true happiness comes from within, it comes from intimately connecting with others and having deep and meaningful*

Foreword

relationships, it comes from doing work that you are passionate about, it comes from being generous towards others, but most of all, happiness simply comes by being at peace with who you are and knowing that you are enough no matter what the external circumstances."

Enjoy the book and use it to do the one thing that will catapult you forward, join a men's group.

Graham Reid Phoenix

November 2016

The historic ascent of humanity, taken as a whole, may be summarized as a succession of victories of consciousness over blind forces—in nature, in society, in man himself.

Leon Trotsky

Chapter 1
A Shift in Male Consciousness

I'd like you to take a moment and think about a very big question. When I ask the question, take a moment and really think about it before you give your answer. Are you ready? Here it is. What do you believe is the greatest challenge facing our world today?

I told you it was a big question, so, do you have an answer?

If you watch our current media you may have answered that the greatest challenge facing our world is one of these things:

Terrorism

Poverty

Racism

Violence

Global Warming

Corporate Corruption

Homophobia

Religious Fundamentalism

But what if I told you that our greatest challenge isn't even on this list? What if I told you that our greatest challenge has very little to do with this list but actually is the reason that this list exists?

So before I give my answer, I would like to let you know that this is my opinion and my opinion only. I have come to this conclusion as a result of more than 25 years of research and after writing several books on this particular topic. Would you like to know what I believe is the greatest challenge facing our world? Here it is. I believe the greatest challenge facing our world today is to:

Redefine manhood and create a new paradigm of masculinity on the planet.

So why do I believe this is the greatest challenge? Let's break it down!

If you take a look at the list above, you may notice that men contribute overwhelmingly to these problems. Most terrorists are men, men are responsible for the overwhelming majority of violence in our culture, most corporate CEOs are men and the truth is most religious fundamentalist preachers are men. Based on these facts, it should be easy to recognize that men create a lot of challenges in the world.

So the question we must ask ourselves is, are men the real problem?

Despite what I just shared, I believe the answer is a resounding no. At the heart of these problems aren't men, at the heart of these problems is an antiquated paradigm of masculinity that men are trapped in and they unfortunately aren't even conscious of it. So in order to remove the challenges I mentioned earlier, we must create a new culture or paradigm of masculinity that helps men awaken to new ways of being and relating as men.

Chapter 1 ~ A Shift in Male Consciousness

This is much easier said than done. During the last twenty years or so that I've been writing about men's work and attempting to help men improve their lives, I have been accused of male bashing and selling out men. I've been called a "mangina", a wimp, a sensitive new age guy and a man who is basically out of touch with reality. But despite these attacks, I stand firm on my contention that the key to resolving the overwhelming majority of problems facing our world is to redefine manhood and create a new paradigm of masculinity.

So how do we do this? How do we get men to embrace this new idea and join this new revolution that is designed to make their lives better? How do we get men to open up and realize that there is a better way to embrace masculinity that will support them in being happier, more fulfilled and passionate about their lives?

The key to doing this is to create a shift in male consciousness.

What I mean by that is we must challenge men to examine their deeply held thoughts, feelings and subconscious beliefs about what it means to be a man and become aware of the erroneous internal dialog men sometimes have with themselves. It is an inside job, which encompasses addressing our beliefs, emotions, judgments and assumptions about what it means to be a man. It begins with a single man and then expands to groups of men and then cities of men and then countries of men and ultimately the entire planet.

In the words of the great philosopher Lao Tzu, "If you want to remove the darkness from your world you must first be willing to remove the darkness from within yourself." So this shift in male consciousness is the removal of darkness within ourselves so that we can ultimately remove it from our world. I am so committed to making this happen I have even started my own publishing company with the sole intent and purpose of transforming the world one man at a time.

In case you haven't noticed yet, I consider myself to be an irrepressible optimist. Despite what you may see or have concluded from watching the media, it is my fervent belief that the world is on a trajectory of positivity and the future is filled with unlimited possibilities for those people who are willing to take 100% responsibility for their lives and are willing to capitalize on the technological and informational advances that are currently being made around the globe.

Amazingly, most people do not share my sense of optimism, especially when it comes to men. On the surface it appears that men are like the old dogs that can't learn new tricks, but I on the other hand believe that you can teach old dogs new tricks and that is the reason for my optimism.

The primary reason I remain optimistic about men is because I believe men are going through an evolutionary cycle. This evolutionary cycle is not based on Darwin's theory of evolution but rather my own theory of how men are evolving. My theories are based on my own research and are actually my own personal observations, opinions and beliefs about men. I am not going to provide you with scientific statistics (I really dislike statistics) or scientifically substantiated proof. I am simply going to share my perceptions of the status of men in society and where I believe men are headed.

It is my opinion and belief that there are five stages of evolution that males have gone through. (I shared these stages in my previous book,

A New Conversation With Men, in 2008.) As I share these five stages, simply ask yourself if they make sense to you. Try to take a global view, because this evolutionary process is global. Men around the globe have gone through and continue to go through this process. It does not matter what country you're from or what part of the world you were born into. The five stages of evolution for males are:

The Caveman Male

The Warrior Male

The Religious Male

The Scientific Male

The Authentic Male

The Caveman Male

This is where it all began. The caveman male had three basic responsibilities. First, he was responsible for securing shelter. His job was to find a cave that kept him out of the elements and provided protection from those carnivorous animals that were trying to have him for dinner. Second, he was responsible for finding a mate to insure the continuation of the species. Third, he was responsible for feeding and protecting his family. It was his job to literally bring home the bacon (or whatever prehistoric equivalent there was to a pig) and at the same time make sure he did not become a meal himself. His primary objective was simply survival.

With the exception of inclement weather and the occasional run in with saber-tooth tigers, the caveman male had a pretty good life. He did everything on instinct and relied solely on his intuition and gut feelings. That is how he survived and thrived. These instincts and gut feelings led him to amazing discoveries, which propelled him to evolve into the warrior male.

The Warrior Male

The warrior male had the same responsibilities as the caveman male, but the warrior male had developed language. Language allowed the warrior male to expand on the discoveries of the caveman male and develop new tools and new weapons that the caveman male did not have access to.

With the addition of language, the warrior male began communicating in new and different ways with his surroundings. This new form of communication allowed him to expand his awareness and ultimately led him to conclude that he was different from anyone who did not look like him or behave like him. With this way of viewing the world, his primary objective became conquering anyone who he perceived to be different. This led to war and separation amongst men. After several hundred years, the warrior male had to continue to evolve to insure the continuation of the species and therefore the religious male was formed.

The Religious Male

As a way of removing some of the violent and inhumane acts against men, the religious male was born. This was the result of the emergence of highly evolved human beings that taught new ways of being men in society. These spiritual masters demonstrated that it was possible to live in peace and harmony with each other, and they provided spiritual principles that taught men how to live together. Unfortunately, their teachings were sometimes misinterpreted and abused, and they became the foundation for more wars and killings in the name of the spiritual teachers. Eventually men began to reject the teachings of the spiritual masters and started to rely strictly on science and intellectual understanding to try to solve people's problems. This lead to new technological breakthroughs which created the next step in male evolution: the scientific male.

The Scientific Male

The scientific male relies solely on his intellect and science to solve problems. He is constantly looking outside himself for answers and relies on technology to help fix whatever ails him. He realizes that he has access to things like television and the Internet, and he places most of his faith in material things. He exhibits qualities of the caveman male, the warrior male, and the religious male, but his primary focus is on "external" things. As a result, he has experienced emptiness and disconnection which is now propelling him towards new ways of being a man. He is tired of looking for external validation and is seeking something real, something that he can invest his soul into, something with meaning and fulfillment. The only way he can experience this is to evolve into the authentic male.

The Authentic Male

The authentic male is the culmination of all aspects of being male. It is taking the best of all aspects and combining them into a highly aware, intuitive man who is completely conscious and awake to who he is as a man. The authentic male knows who he is, and he is able to be authentic and transparent in all of his interactions with others. He recognizes that there is a part of him that is like the caveman male that must be responsible for providing shelter and food for him and his family. He knows that he has a warrior's spirit that encourages him to challenge his own fears and move through them without hesitation. He embraces his religious male by developing a spiritual connection that nurtures his soul, and he supports his scientific male by expanding his intellect and making use of current technology.

But ultimately he knows that he needs absolutely nothing outside of himself to be validated. He is the authentic male and he knows without question that he is lovable and acceptable just the way he is without any external thing. He recognizes and accepts the fact that he is not perfect, and simultaneously he knows that in actuality he is perfect as a result of his imperfections. He is able to live and love deeply, and he is committed to having and maintaining relationships that nurture his mind, body and spirit. He refuses to accept mediocrity in any form, and he strives to become the best man he can be. His relationships are his highest priority, and therefore he measures his success by the depth of his relationships.

This is the reason why I am so optimistic about men and the future. I strongly believe that men are evolving into the authentic male and in doing so we will create the new paradigm of masculinity that I've been speaking about. This evolutionary process is driving a shift in male consciousness that will usher in new ways of being and relating for men, which I believe will ultimately assist in the eradication of the majority of social ills that currently plague our world.

Chapter 1 ~ A Shift in Male Consciousness

This book is written to help facilitate this process and the fact that you're reading it right now confirms that you are a part of this evolution.

So let me welcome and congratulate you on engaging in a new paradigm of masculinity that is shifting the male consciousness on the planet to make it a better place.

Healing may not be so much about getting better, as about letting go of everything that isn't you—all of the expectations, all of the beliefs—and becoming who you are.

Rachel Naomi Remen

Chapter 2
Men's Emotional Healing

Incident #1. On June 12, 2016, a person killed 49 people and injured 53 others inside a nightclub in Orlando, Florida.

Incident #2. On June 17, 2015, a person killed 9 people in a church in Charleston, South Carolina.

Incident #3. On December 14, 2012, a person killed 20 children and six adults at an elementary school in Newton, Connecticut.

What do these three incidents have in common? Before I share the obvious answer, I would like to share an article posted on a social media site titled DearFellowWhitePeople that sums it up pretty well. The article was written in response to incident #1.

"I think it's worth noting that before any of us knew what the race of the shooter was, we all knew he was a man. Because nothing says toxic masculinity like a homophobic hate crime. He could have been a white Westboro Baptist or a brown Muslim, or any number of other possible combinations of conservative religion and skin tone. But a mass shooting at a gay bar was always going to be committed by a man. So let's start talking about the global problems of toxic masculinity and homophobia, and what we can do collectively to fix them, and skip the finger pointing at other cultures when we know our house is far from clean."

DEARFELLOWWHITEPEOPLE

The answer to the question as to what the three incidents have in common is that the perpetuator of each violent act was a man who used a gun to take innocent people's lives. This is an undeniable fact, not an opinion. There are lots of speculations behind their motivations but the undisputed truth is that they were men with guns who killed innocent people.

After incident #1, here are a few of the headlines that dominated the media. "Act of Terror Kills 50 At Nightclub," "50 killed at gay nightclub in Fla.," "A Night of Terror in Orlando," "Islamist Terrorist Kills 50" "Praising Isis, Gunman Attacks Gay Nightclub, Leaving 50 Dead In Worst Shooting On US Soil."

These headlines suggest the motive for the killings were driven by Islamic religious ideologies and therefore the killer was a terrorist. But is that the true cause of this violent act? Is a person's commitment to his religion or ideology the direct cause that drives a person to commit murder? Was his hatred of homosexuals the real reason he went into a gay bar and committed this horrendous crime?

In incident #2, a white male gunman goes into a black church and kills 9 black people and says that he wanted to create a race war. He is then labeled a racist and the conclusion is that it is his hatred of black people that caused him to commit this unimaginable crime.

In incident #3, the gunman goes into an elementary school and takes the lives of 20 elementary school age children. The media labels him as mentally disturbed and suggests that the reason he committed this heinous act was because of mental illness.

Whenever there is a massacre or the loss of multiple people's lives in our society, we generally use these three explanations for the killing: it is either an act of religious terrorism, racism or mental illness. But is that the right answer? Are these three things the real reason people are killing other people?

To answer this question I will go back to the quote from DearFellowWhitePeople: *"So let's start talking about the global problems of toxic masculinity and homophobia, and what we can do collectively to fix them, and skip the finger pointing at other cultures when we know our house is far from clean."*

Herein lies the real problem as I see it. It is the global problem of toxic masculinity. But what exactly does toxic masculinity mean? And how do you fix it?

As a result of the research and studying I've done over the past twenty years, I have concluded that toxic masculinity is driven by five illusions of manhood that men hold on to that cause the overwhelming majority of pain and suffering in their lives. These illusions have been perpetuated through our families, our cultures and our media for hundreds of years. It is the collective consciousness of men around the globe and it affects men of all races, religions or economic status.

To fix the toxic masculinity that permeates the planet, we must first wake up from these illusions for ourselves and then support other men in doing the same. (I first discussed these illusions in my previous book, A New Conversation With Men, in 2008.)

In order to break free from these illusions a man must first become aware that they even exist. So I would like to share these five illusions with you now:

1. To be a man you must be non-emotional and disconnected.
2. To be a man you must use sexual conquest as a gauge for manhood.
3. To be a man you must have status, position and power.
4. To be a man you must have money and material possessions.
5. To be a man you must win at all costs and compete against other men.

These five illusions are the foundation of all pain and misery in a man's life and are the indirect foundation of most violent acts. If you will take a moment and really examine them, I believe you will see what I mean. To give you a better understanding of how these illusions affect your life, I will now break them down and explain each one individually.

1. To be a man you must be non-emotional and disconnected.

I believe that this is the greatest illusion of all. All other illusions are actually built on top of this one. In our society, males are conditioned and taught from a very young age that it's not okay to feel. We are given the messages that to feel and express those feelings is somehow weak, or worse, feminine. Therefore we start accepting this illusion even as little boys. Think about the powerful messages you may have received as a young boy, things like, "Big boys don't cry," "Stop being a baby," and "Don't act like a sissy." These are the beginnings of the acceptance of this illusion. What actually occurs is that we begin to shut down our emotions, and the only way to cope is to express through our intellect. We stop expressing how we feel, and we begin expressing what we think. Of course there is absolutely nothing wrong with thinking. Using our intellect is an integral and necessary aspect of our humanity, but without our emotions, we become empty, hollow automatons that miss out on the most important aspect of our lives.

This illusion is powerful because, as men, we accept that the only appropriate feelings we should express are the negative ones. If you pay close attention, you should notice that it's absolutely acceptable for a man to express anger and rage in our society without being accused of being less than a man, but if a man expresses joy, sadness or fear then his masculinity will always be questioned.

A good example of this is a television interview I watched with Terrell Owens, who was a wide receiver for the Dallas Cowboys football team. After the Cowboys suffered an emotional loss to the New York Giants, Terrell was defending his friend and quarterback Tony Romo. In the interview, Terrell began to cry as he openly shares how unfair the media was being to his friend. It was obvious that he was deeply saddened by the loss, but he was also saying just how much he cared for his friend. As a result of this interview, his masculinity was immediately challenged. The media went into frenzy about Terrell's emotional interview. Some of the sportscasters accused him of being weak and overly sensitive while others even questioned his sexuality by implying that he might be gay.

The question I pose to you is why is it so unacceptable in our society for a man to be emotional? Does it really make us less than men if we are comfortable expressing our feelings and wear our hearts on our sleeves? Who decided that women could be emotional but not men?

This is accepted in our society because we are trapped in the illusion that men are supposed to be non-emotional and disconnected. It is an illusion that has been passed down for generations, and the time has come for us to wake up. When a man is trapped in this illusion, he loses his ability to truly experience life the way it was meant to be. Without his emotions he will miss out on the most important aspects of his life. His joy, passion, creativity, intuition, connection with his spouse, children, even his faith are all connected to his ability to feel, so it is important that we break free from this illusion and create a new paradigm in which men are comfortable expressing their emotions openly and honestly without fear of having our masculinity challenged.

If you look deeply into the cause of all violence, this illusion is the reason it exists. It isn't primarily religious terrorism, racism or even mental illness (although mental illness can definitely influence violent acts) that causes a person to commit violent acts; it is the emotion of anger, which in most cases is the result of unresolved emotional pain. If we truly want to get to the core reason of why a person commits violent acts, it could be summed up into this simple quote: "emotional pain will cause a person to do irrational things." It's been said that only a hurt person will hurt another person and I completely agree with that statement. Until we as a country/world accept this fact and figure out how to alleviate the emotional pain within the heart and soul of the people who commit these violent acts, things will never change. We can pass legislation on gun control and create more penalties and jail time for abusers but it will still not remove the anger in their hearts, which once again is the core reason for the violence in the first place.

What is truly needed is compassion, empathy and understanding for men to help them deal with this powerful illusion. When we teach men how to deal with their emotions appropriately, I believe we will begin to see the eradication of the majority of the senseless acts of violence that currently plagues our world.

2. To be a man you must use sexual conquest as a gauge for manhood.

This is one of the most destructive illusions perpetuated throughout our society and the world. This illusion contributes to teenage pregnancy, divorce, the rape culture, sexually transmitted diseases, and all sorts of violence. I cannot pinpoint when this illusion began, but I would assume that it has been around since the beginning of time. It really doesn't matter when it started; the question we must ask ourselves is how we can we end it. With the over proliferation of sexual images and the "sex sells" mentality of our media, it's no wonder so many men get trapped in this illusion.

Think back to your youth and see if you remember how prevalent this illusion was, especially during your younger days. Do you remember when you were young and the only thing you thought about was sex? As a teenager, our minds and our hormones were obsessed with the prospect of having sex. If we are really honest with ourselves, we will recognize that almost everything we did in some way led to us to try to attract the opposite sex so that we could engage in the act of sex. We bought our cars to try to attract girls. We played sports hoping that it would attract girls. We bought clothes and kept our hair perfect in hopes of attracting girls. We made money to impress and attract girls. So why were we so obsessed with girls? Because we wanted to have sex! We all believed that by having sex we would validate our manhood, and our friends would cheer for us, and we would be happy and fulfilled. So if we weren't having sex, we usually lied about it just to make sure that we maintained the illusion that we were real men. If we weren't having sex and maintaining this illusion, then we usually felt inadequate and somehow inferior as young men.

Now I would like you to fast forward to the present. If you will take a moment and ask yourself the same questions you will see that most of us as men are still trapped in the same illusion. We buy cars to attract women. We play sports to attract women. We buy clothes and keep our hair perfect to attract women. We make money and spend money to attract and impress women. So why are we so obsessed with attracting women? Because we want to have sex with women! And when we aren't having sex with women we're usually lying about it to our friends. Can you see the insanity in this? Sexual conquest does not make you a man. It is only an illusion and a temporary fix to your unhappiness. If you are using sex as a gauge for manhood, you are trapped in a vicious cycle of addiction and denial.

3. To be a man you must have status, position and power.

Have you ever noticed how our society adores celebrities, sports figures and executives? We are taught that, "He who has the gold makes the rules," which implies that the more money you have the "better" you are as a person. The implication is that somehow men who are wealthier or who have higher societal status are somehow "superior" to other men. This is definitely an illusion. The truth of the matter is that monetary wealth does not make you a better man. It may in some ways make your life easier, but it definitely does not make a man superior to other men. The sad part of it is that too many men accept this illusion and they spend all of their energy trying to move up the societal ladder to validate themselves. They invest all of their time and energy in trying to gain titles and labels, while in reality they feel empty and unfulfilled. The way that they try to compensate for this emptiness is by acting "superior" even though they really aren't.

I must admit that I was definitely caught in this illusion twenty years ago. Although I did not consider myself to be superior to any other man, I did believe that attaining the title of "Manager" would somehow validate me as a man. Although I did not recognize it at the time, my ambition and drive was actually fueled by my own insecurities about being a man. In my mind, climbing the corporate ladder and becoming successful was a way to prove to myself that I was competent and intelligent. Unfortunately, even after I made it to the top, I still felt the same insecurities. Even though I projected the façade of being in control and in charge, there was a part of me that was a frightened little boy simply trying to find his way home.

Too many men are currently caught in this illusion of manhood. You can recognize them by their big egos and their arrogance. They parade around town flashing their titles at you and trying to get the external validation they so desperately need. On the outside they may appear to have it all together, but on the inside they are wounded little boys doing the best they can to maintain their charade.

4. To be a man you must have money and material possessions.

This illusion is the reason men spend billions upon billions of dollars buying "stuff." Too many of us believe that if we just buy the right house, the right car, the right watch or the right clothes then we will be viewed as men and we will gain approval from our friends. This is the reason why so many of us feel empty and discontented: because we have bought into the illusion that if we accumulate enough "stuff" we will feel fulfilled. Nothing could be further from the truth. This illusion is why so many of us try to "Keep up with the Joneses."

As I think about this illusion, I'm reminded of my high school days when I purchased my first car, a 1969 Ford Mustang that I absolutely loved. But it wasn't the freedom that came from owning my own car that excited me: it was the fact that in my mind I had now become a man. Of course, I was only seventeen at the time and still living at home, but in my mind I had graduated from adolescence and moved into manhood. (This just goes to show you how this particular illusion really kicks in around our formative high school years.)

Another way that I bought into this illusion was by pretending that I had lots of money even when I didn't. I remember keeping a big wad of cash in my pocket at all times, and I would always have a twenty or a fifty dollar bill on top with lots of one dollar bills on the bottom. Whenever I was out with my friends, I would pull out my wad of cash and pretend that I had a lot more money than I actually did. Since most of my friends didn't have jobs or money, I was always seen as "The Man" to my peers. This was definitely a big boost for my ego but it caused me to fall deeper and deeper into the illusion.

These are just two examples of the things some of us as men do when we are trapped in this illusion. Sadly, there are currently lots of men out there today who are still doing the things that I did in high school. (Are you one of them?) They are the ones who have become trapped in the illusion that they must have money and material things to be a man, and I can assure you that they are paying a significant price in terms of their emotional, psychological and spiritual well being.

5. To be a man you must win at all costs and compete against other men.

This is probably the least recognized of all the illusions. Although we seldom talk openly about this, there is an unspoken male law that says that we are supposed to always compete against each other. This can be witnessed on a large scale by corporate corruption. When a man's ego gets inflated, he will do any and everything to "stay on top." All rational thinking will go out the window if a man thinks that his competitor is getting ahead of him. Our business schools teach us that being competitive is the foundation of success, but they will not teach you about the consequences of this overly competitive, macho position that too many men fall victim to.

A perfect example of this on a small scale is an experience I had as a salesman in a hardware store. One day I sold a customer a very expensive barbeque grill. The customer wanted to make sure that it had all of the latest technology, and he wanted it to be the "best." I worked with him for a couple of days until I finally put together the grill of his dreams. As he walked out of the store, his final comment to me was, "Thanks for helping me put together such an awesome grill.

My neighbor is going to be green with envy."

A couple of days later a gentleman shows up and asks to speak to me about purchasing a grill. He specifically asked for me because his neighbor told him that I was very helpful. He raved about how awesome his neighbor's grill was and he said he wanted to purchase one just like it. But then he added that he wanted to make sure that it had at least one feature that his neighbors grill did not have. He did not care what the feature was - as a matter of fact, he even mentioned that he probably wouldn't use the new feature - he simply wanted to make sure that it was better than his neighbor's grill.

This is what happens when you get caught in this illusion. You will do irrational things and then rationalize them by saying you work hard for your money and you deserve to have the best. Of course, there is nothing wrong with wanting the best for yourself, but when you get trapped in this illusion, you will ultimately experience emptiness.

These are the five illusions of manhood that are perpetuated throughout our society and the world. They are the root cause of "toxic masculinity". It is absolutely imperative that you recognize these illusions and not be trapped by them.

To assist you in breaking free from these illusions I would now like to share five concrete things you can do to break free from them.

1. You must be willing to become aware that the illusion exists.

This is always the most difficult and challenging step, and at the same time it is always the first step. As soon as you become aware that you are trapped in the illusion, you have already begun waking up from it. Take some time and reflect on these illusions and then write down the one that resonates the most for you. By writing down the illusion it will begin to lose its grip on you. Imagine the illusion as internal darkness and your awareness as eternal light. By shining the light onto the darkness the darkness disappears. Your awareness is the light which will remove the darkness. Challenge yourself to become aware of the illusion you may be caught in.

2. You must be willing to be transformed by the renewing of your mind.

This is what I mean by having a shift in male consciousness. It means becoming aware of old belief systems, thought patterns and assumptions in your mind that may no longer be working for you. By changing your internal dialog you lay the foundation for new ways of being a man. Think of your mind as a garden and all of your thoughts as seeds. Whatever seed (thought) you plant has to grow. If you are planting negative seeds, guess what grows? If you are planting positive seeds, what do you think will sprout up? Transforming your mind means that you make a conscious effort in recognizing what types of seeds you are planting. The more conscious you become, the more likely you are to plant positive seeds. This also means that you become conscious of all of the things that you are allowing to be planted in your mind. This means that you should limit your exposure to all of the negative seeds that are planted by our media. So do yourself a favor and disconnect from too much television.

3. You must be willing to heal and reconnect to your emotions.

This is definitely our greatest challenge as men. As I mentioned, we are conditioned not to feel, but it is our responsibility to go against the societal conditioning and become courageous enough to begin our emotional-healing process. Until you learn to heal and feel, there will always be something missing in your life. In order to heal, you must follow the next step.

4. You must seek support.

You must understand that you cannot do this alone. I understand how difficult it is for men to seek support, but the fact remains: you must seek help. I don't care if you go to therapy, join a men's group, join AA, or go to a church group. It is important that you surround yourself with like-minded men who can support and challenge you to become the best man you can be. Gaining the courage to seek support is a surefire way to help you break free from any of these illusions.

I have come to believe that the three most difficult words for a man to say are: "I need help". The reason this is so difficult is because our current masculine culture has conditioned us to believe that it is a sign of weakness to do so. It is not a sign of weakness but a sign of strength to be able to ask for help but rest assured that it can be extremely difficult because of our current toxic masculinity culture.

To help remove this toxic masculinity culture and hopefully support you in possibly seeking support if needed, I would like to share an article I wrote a while back titled 'Men's Emotional Healing'. The intention for writing it was to remove the negative stigma men feel about asking for help and to hopefully provide some insights on how difficult it can be to take the first steps toward healing. My hope is that the article will provide you with some insights about the challenges you may face and to also let you know that there should be no shame in seeking support and when you do, your life will definitely take a turn for the better.

Once again, it's titled 'Men's Emotional Healing':

In 1989, I was experiencing a series of traumatic experiences that were beginning to take their toll. My divorce and separation from my kids were extremely painful and had begun to negatively impact my life. I had slipped into a deep state of depression and was barely able to function on a daily basis. As my depression deepened, I went into isolation in which I literally shut myself off from the outside world. Although I was able to go to work and function in that capacity, I was completely disconnected from any social settings. I was not dating. I did not socialize with my friends. I had difficulty sleeping. I would rarely eat, and I had begun to lose weight, which was rare for me, being a former personal trainer who took excellent care of my physical body. After several months, I began to have fleeting thoughts of suicide, and it appeared that my situation was hopeless.

In an effort to alleviate some of the pain, I begin to read books dealing with depression. I could see myself in some of the stories as I read them. I definitely had all of the symptoms of depression, and I knew that I had to deal with it head on if I ever wanted to get my life back on track. After reading several books, I realized that I was still deeply depressed and had not really begun to deal with the issues that were causing my depression. Instinctively I knew that I needed help, and I decided that I would go to therapy.

After making the decision to get help, another series of challenges surfaced. First of all, how was I going to find a therapist? How would I know which one to choose? What if the therapist couldn't help me? Would I be able to change? Could therapy "fix" me? What about the money? I was completely broke and definitely could not pay someone to listen to my problems. What was I going to do? These are just a few of the questions that were going through my mind. My greatest fear was wondering what would happen if my employees found out. As a manager, I was considered the leader, and I definitely did not want to appear weak in front of my co-workers. I believed that I needed to keep this a secret so that I would not lose the respect of my employees. In addition, I did not want my superiors to know because I thought I might lose my job if they found out.

After a few months of agonizing over these questions, I knew that I had to take the chance and try therapy. I didn't have any other choice. It was seek help or die. There was no gray area. I decided that I definitely wanted to live, and I somehow gained the courage to go to the therapist's office.

My first attempt at therapy did not go well. I walked into the therapist's office and pretended that I was seeking information for a friend. I'm sure the people there knew this, but they allowed me to walk out with some of their brochures and a phone number to their suicide hotline. To be honest, I was absolutely terrified. Although I was scared, deep

Chapter 2 ~ Men's Emotional Healing

down I knew that I would have to find the courage to try again. I waited a few days and tried a different therapist's office. This time I had a completely different result. As I walked into the office, I believe the receptionist picked up on my fear. I had begun asking her questions about depression and whether or not they had any books that I could read. All of a sudden, a therapist walked out and began asking me questions.

"May I help you?" she asked.

"Not really, I'm just looking for a little information about depression."

"Are you depressed?"

"I'm not really sure," I answered.

"Why don't you come inside and let's talk a little. Is that all right?"

"I guess so."

As I followed her into her office, it felt as if my heart was going to jump out of my chest. I was so nervous and afraid that I was literally dripping with sweat. She obviously picked up on this and began to put my mind at ease.

"What is your name?"

"Michael."

"Well, Michael, I can sense that you are a little nervous, so let me start by asking what I can do to help you. Is there anything I can do for you?"

"Well, maybe. I have been doing some research about depression, and I think I'm depressed, but I'm really not sure."

"Do you feel depressed?"

"Based on what I've read so far, I think I am. But to be completely honest, I'm not sure I know exactly what depression is supposed to feel like. Does that make any sense to you?"

"It makes a lot of sense to me. Unfortunately, most men do not recognize how they feel. Men have been conditioned to disconnect from their emotions, and that makes it extremely difficult for men to express how they really feel. Most men will tell you what they think, but they usually do not know how they feel. You apparently fit into this category."

"I'm not sure if I really understand what you are saying, but a part of me thinks that you are right."

"You just validated the point I made. You are currently speaking from an intellectual perspective instead of an emotional one. It sounds as if you are disconnected from your emotions."

"Let's assume that you are right. If I am disconnected from my emotions, how do I get reconnected? Do you have any books on how to do this?"

"Unfortunately you cannot reconnect to your emotions by reading books. In order for you to reconnect, you have to relearn how to feel. This can be accomplished through therapy with me or any trained therapist."

"I really don't understand what you mean. But if I decide to relearn how to feel, how long will it take?

"I really can't answer that question. It's really up to you and how committed you are to doing the work."

"What do you mean 'doing the work'? What kind of work is involved?"

"In the therapeutic community, we use the word 'work' because it takes a considerable amount of effort to heal yourself so that you can reconnect with your emotions. Doing the work means that you become willing to opening yourself up on an emotional level. This can be quite difficult at times."

"Well, I believe I'm ready. I'm really tired of being alone and I definitely want to experience some fun in my life again. I think I can do this, so how much will it cost?"

"I operate on a sliding scale based on your ability to pay. The most important thing is for you to make the commitment to yourself to heal, and we can address the money issue at a later date. Are you ready to begin? Let's set up a date and time for you to begin your healing."

"I just want to thank you for being so nice and understanding. The truth is, I was about to run out of your office before you showed up. Now I am really glad that I came because I really believe that you can help me."

"That is a great attitude to have. I'm glad that you trust me enough to work with you. Just remember that I can guide you, but you must be willing to do the work. As long as you believe that you can heal, I can assure you that you will. Just stay committed and trust the process, and you will be just fine. The truth is you have already done the hard part by showing up today. It takes an incredible amount of courage to be here, and I'm proud of you for taking the first step."

As I left the therapist's office that day, I knew that I had just taken the biggest step of my life. I did not know what to expect, but I knew that I was willing to do whatever it took to heal my emotions and relearn how to feel. I became committed to my own healing and I can now say that I am emotionally healed and connected to my authentic self. As the therapist mentioned, it was not easy, but it was definitely possible. It has been one of the most challenging yet most fulfilling journeys of my life. I cannot put into words the joy I feel on a regular basis as a result of doing my emotional work. My relationships now work, my creativity and sense of reverence is enhanced, my love of nature has been rekindled, and my professional life is rewarding and fulfilling. I took the road less traveled, and it has made all the difference in the world for me.

I wanted to share this story because there is such a negative stigma about men and therapy and I believe it's time for a new conversation. In this new conversation, men will recognize the importance of healing their emotions, and they will invest the effort to do their healing work. When we learn to support each other in our growth we can remove the fear and stigma of being emotionally vulnerable, which will ultimately result in us being happier human beings. I believe that this is the most important work in which men can participate and we must begin supporting each other through this process. If we gain the courage to do this work, we will see a decline in domestic violence, child abuse, alcoholism and random acts of violence. The time has come for a new conversation about our emotional healing. Are you willing to join the conversation?

5. You must develop a spiritual connection that works for you.

This does not necessarily mean that you have to join a church or other religious organization. It means that you must come to your own understanding that there is a power greater than yourself in the universe. By connecting to this power, it will give you strength, faith and courage to break free from the illusions and live a more rewarding and fulfilling life. Once you develop this connection, it is your responsibility to nurture it and insure that you stay connected to it.

~ ~ ~ ~ ~

Despite the negativity and pessimism of our media I remain optimistic that we can overcome the multiplicity of challenges facing our world. Supporting men in waking up from these illusions can help eradicate a lot of the senseless acts of violence and general dysfunction that seems to permeate our news. The key is to support men in shifting their consciousness and engaging in their emotional healing work and creating a new paradigm of masculinity on the planet.

It will not happen through legislation or regulation but through the willingness of men to heal their hearts and do their emotional healing work.

That is the real spiritual awakening, when something emerges from within you that is deeper than who you thought you were. So, the person is still there, but one could almost say that something more powerful shines through the person.

Eckhart Tolle

Chapter 3
The Awakened Male

My experience has taught me that there are only two things that will cause a man to "wake up" or get support in making a change in their lives. The first thing is pain, and I believe 90% of men fall into this category. The second thing is called divine discontent, which is an internal knowing that something about our lives just isn't right and we have a "feeling" that our lives could actually be better.

The sad part is that most men do not even recognize that they are in pain until something devastating comes along that insures that they actually experience and feel the pain they were not aware they were in. This pain takes lots of different forms. Divorce or relationship breakups, illnesses, addictions, depression, job loss or personal tragedy are all different forms of pain that usually provide us with a wake-up call that something needs to change in our lives.

For me it was my divorce. Although my divorce didn't catch me by surprise (I had been unhappy in my marriage for awhile), it was the painful catalyst that caused me to acknowledge that I was in pain. As painful as it was, it turned out to be the best thing that ever happened to me as I look back in retrospect.

The reason I say that is because after my divorce, I was forced to look deeply within my own heart and mind to figure out what the real cause of my pain was. What I found out was that it really wasn't my divorce that had caused me most of my pain; it was something much deeper that I had to figure out. This caused me to begin an inner journey that allowed me to heal my heart and alleviate the pain I was in but more importantly, it guided me to discover who I really am and what my purpose in life is.

Before I share some insights about my journey, I wanted to share an article I wrote that serves as a perfect metaphor for why so many men struggle with being happy in their lives. I wrote this piece after thinking about how difficult it can be as a man sometimes and I think this article really summarizes why it can be so difficult for men to "wake up" and become genuinely happy with their lives. It's called 'The Rollercoaster'.

The Rollercoaster

I had heard a lot about the rollercoaster. Initially I didn't want to go and see it, but everyone kept saying, "You have to check it out and get on it. It will be so much fun."

Reluctantly, I went to see it. It was intriguing and enticing and it looked like fun.

> "You have to get on it!" everyone said.
>
> "I'm not sure that I want to."
>
> "But everyone loves getting on the rollercoaster," they said.
>
> "I don't think I'll like it."
>
> "Go ahead and try it. You'll like it," everyone said.

Chapter 3 ~ The Awakened Male

So I tried it.

At the beginning it was fun. Going round and round and up and down with friends who also seemed to be having fun was initially enjoyable.

But after a short while, I got bored and tired. I didn't want to ride it any more. I decided that I wanted to get off.

> "You can't get off," everyone said.
>
> "But I'm ready to."
>
> "No one gets off the rollercoaster once they get on."
>
> "Why not?"
>
> "They just don't."
>
> "But I'm ready to get off."
>
> "Why not ride it a little longer and see if you change your mind?" they said.
>
> "Okay, I'll try it a little longer."

Round and round, up and down I went pretending that I was enjoying myself.

But after a while I began to get angry. I was tired of the rollercoaster and I realized that I shouldn't have got on it in the first place. I wanted to get off, but I didn't know how.

> "I'm really sick of this rollercoaster. I want to get off right now."
>
> "We're sorry but you must stay on the rollercoaster. That's the rule."

"Well, I guess I'm going to have to break the rule because I'm about to get off."

"But if you break the rule no one will like you and you will probably get hurt," they said.

"I don't care about anyone else. I want to get off now. Who can I talk to about getting off this thing?"

"No one knows how to get off," they said.

"I'm sure someone knows. I just have to find them."

"It's been said that only a few people have ever got off this rollercoaster. And no one really knows what happened to them. Some believe that people have even been killed trying to get off. Why take that risk?"

"At this point I'm willing to take that risk. I don't care what people think or what people are going to say. I refuse to keep going round and round and getting nowhere on this thing, and I must do something to get off."

I didn't know what to do, but I knew that I couldn't stay on the rollercoaster. I needed a plan and I needed it soon. I felt as though I was dying and I really wanted to live again.

But what about the risk? What if what they say is true? What if I really can't get off or what if I get killed trying to get off?

At this point, I decide that I have only one choice. And that choice is to live. I don't know what is going to happen, but I know if I stay on this thing I'm already dead. I have to trust my inner instincts and take the chance and simply jump off. I'm not sure where I'll land or if I'll

Chapter 3 ~ The Awakened Male

get hurt or even die, but I just know that I have to jump.

So, despite what everyone else was saying and the fear and uncertainty I felt, I took a deep breath and jumped. As my body was hurled through the air uncontrollably, surprisingly I felt a deep sense of calm and inner peace, and then I did exactly what I intuitively knew I could do—I flew!

~ ~ ~ ~ ~

This story serves as a perfect metaphor for masculinity in society today. Too many men are trapped on the societal rollercoaster and they don't know how to get off. Some are afraid of what others might think if they get off while others are simply too afraid to take a risk and do something different with their lives. Either way, they stay stuck on the rollercoaster and live lives of quiet desperation with no passion or purpose.

My life is a perfect example of what can happen if you are willing to take the risk and get off of the rollercoaster. During the darkest periods of my life, I had no idea where my life was going or where I might end up. All I was certain of was that I wanted the pain to stop and I wanted to get off of the rollercoaster. I wanted to stop pretending that I was happy and become genuinely happy with my life. So here I am, approximately 25 years later, and I can honestly say to you that right now in this very moment I am happier now than I've ever been. I can also say that the joy I feel on a regular basis today makes all of the pain I experienced earlier in my life worth it.

As mentioned, I decided to jump off of the rollercoaster and in the process I learned I could fly. You too have the ability to fly but you're going to have to gain some courage to do so. To support you in doing so, I'd like to share a few tips to support you in learning how to fly based on the past 25 years of my own growth. Rest assured, if I can overcome all the adversities in my own life, you have everything you need right now to overcome the challenges in your life. Will it be easy? No! Will it be worth it? I can promise you it will!

The first place to start is to recognize that the rollercoaster exists. As mentioned, the rollercoaster is a metaphor for society. The reason we get trapped on it is because we spend an awful lot of time being bombarded with all sorts of erroneous images through our media and we begin believing what the media says is real and will make us happy. For example, if you pay attention to the media, what does it teach us about love? The jewelry companies convince us that if we love someone we buy them diamonds. The floral companies say if you love someone you buy them flowers and the car companies say if you really love someone you buy them a car.

In terms of masculinity, society says to be a man, you must always provide and protect. It teaches us that we are always supposed to be tough and carry the weight of the world on our shoulders. It teaches us that as men we are supposed to never show emotion or appear weak and to win at all costs. We're supposed to attract and conquer women to gain notches on our belts because that's what "real men" do. We are told that he who has the gold makes the rules and the one with the most toys wins. But this is the reason so many of us are so unhappy. We buy into the media's version of happiness and then we can't figure out why our lives are so miserable.

Chapter 3 ~ The Awakened Male

Will Smith said it best when he said: "Too many people spend money they haven't earned, to buy things they don't want, to impress people they don't like."

The reason some of us do this is because we're trapped on the rollercoaster. So, if you truly want to get off, there is a very simple quote that you must commit to memory. Once you fully grasp the depth of this quote, you will have laid the foundation for not only getting off of the rollercoaster, but you've set yourself up to live an extraordinary life. The quote is this:

"If you don't go within, you will always go without."

This is the key to your liberation and freedom.

You may not agree with this or you may not understand it, but here is the universal truth. There is nothing outside of you that will ever make you truly happy. Think about this for a moment. Do you agree?

You see, most people believe that if they had more money, more sex, more material things, more celebrity and recognition then they would be happy. But have you ever seen a story of a celebrity with all of those things but were also strung out on drugs or alcohol and absolutely miserable with their life? Or worse yet, they are so unhappy that they take their own lives just to try to alleviate the pain. The reason this happens is because they were seeking fame instead of fulfillment and fame comes from external things while fulfillment comes from within. Can you see the difference?

You see, going within means you become willing to look at your deepest held beliefs and feelings about who you are. It means being willing to examine how your thoughts and beliefs literally shape your reality because thoughts become things and are extremely powerful. Your thoughts and beliefs about what it means to be a man actually shape your experience of being a man. If you aren't happy as a man, you must be willing to change your thoughts and beliefs about what being a man really means.

As I mentioned earlier, I used to believe being a man meant having the house, the wife, the 2.5 kids, the 401K and the vacations. It wasn't until I had all of those things and then lost them all that I learned that those things really had very little to do with being a man, and they definitely had very little to do with my happiness. Don't get me wrong here. In no way am I saying that there is anything wrong with making money and having nice things. There is nothing wrong with being wealthy and having a beautiful wife and a beautiful house and a job that pays you tons and tons of money. There is nothing wrong with fancy cars and fancy vacations and lots and lots of toys. But if you truly believe that these things are going to make you truly happy, you are definitely mistaken.

Now you may be wondering what I really mean by the quote "You must go within or you will always go without" or you may be wondering exactly how to do that, so let me give you some tips.

A great place to start is by taking a life inventory. The purpose of the inventory is to simply make you aware of areas in your life that can possibly be improved. Once you take the inventory, it gives you a good starting point to begin your own transformational journey.

Here is how it works. Below you will find seven categories of your life that are critical to your success and happiness. The first step is to simply grade these seven areas of your life on a scale of 1 to 10, ten being the highest and best score. Take just a moment and rate these seven areas. Be completely honest with yourself. You can't make a mistake with this test unless you're unwilling to be honest with yourself.

Your personal relationships (Rate the quality and depth of your marriage, intimate relationships, best friends, boyfriends, girlfriends, children etc.)

Score _____

Your intellectual growth (Do you like to read and learn new things?)
Score_____

Your health (Do you smoke? Are you overweight? Do you abuse drugs?) Score_____

Your finances (Are you robbing Peter to pay Paul?)

Score _____

Your emotional awareness (Are you comfortable expressing your feelings? Can you honestly identify them? Are you happy with your life?) Score _____

Your spirituality (Do you have a spiritual connection or practice?)

Score _____

Your sense of purpose (Do you believe your life has a purpose?)

Score _____

As you are rating these categories, pay close attention to your thoughts and feelings. Simply notice what comes up for you as you rate your life. This is not a scientific survey or process. It is simply an opportunity to focus your awareness on your current life situation. It's a simple way of "going within". A lot of men are so focused on their jobs and accumulating material things that they refuse to ask themselves deeper questions. How about you? Are you willing to go within so that you do not have to go without? If you refuse to take the time to fill this out, what does that say about you? It simply says that maybe you are not ready to get off of the rollercoaster, that's all. Maybe you would rather stay stuck in your old ways of being a man. Obviously that is your choice, but I would like to suggest that you reconsider. Hopefully you are reading this book to gain insights to assist you in improving the quality of your life, and if so, here is your opportunity to truly engage in your personal transformation.

Is there a part of you that is saying, "This is silly and irrelevant"? Have you already convinced yourself that your life is fine, and there is no reason for you to do the exercise? Are you rationalizing and analyzing what it all means and judging yourself based on your score? Have you already decided that you simply refuse to do this?

No matter what you have decided to do about this exercise, I'd like to share a simple yet powerful quote with you. "If you keep doing what you've been doing, you'll keep getting what you've always got." Didn't you start reading this book because you believed there was some valuable information in it to help you improve the quality of your life? Are you really committed to yourself and your transformation? Well, here is a great starting point to see just how committed you are.

Chapter 3 ~ The Awakened Male

Be sure to complete the exercise, and I can assure you that you are actively participating in your personal transformation and getting ready to jump off of the rollercoaster.

Now let's take a look at your score. How did you do? Are you surprised by any of your scores? Which areas of your life scored the lowest? How about the highest? If you didn't score 70 points, what can you do to improve your score? The keys to your happiness lie within your willingness to examine these areas and then commit to improving them. But remember, "If you don't go within, you will always go without," which means, if you don't participate in your own transformation, you will go without having dynamic health, great relationships, financial abundance, a fulfilling career, and a spiritual connection that truly nurtures your soul. Transformation is the process of going within. Are you willing to engage in this process?

Unfortunately, most men will wait until they are in a deep, severe crisis before they will begin the process of transformation. Most of us wait until we have ended a relationship or are caught in the middle of a divorce or maybe have lost our job before we realize that something needs to change within us. Sometimes we are swimming in debt or possibly dealing with health issues before we decide to make changes in our lives. I want you to know that all of these events are simply wake-up calls that are designed to help you begin your transformational journey. My intention in this book is to help minimize the challenges and discomfort you experience and help you along the way to a better life. Just remember that you are not alone, and there are literally millions of men who are going through the exact same things that you are going through, men just like you who are ready to get off of the rollercoaster.

Now I would like to share five reasons why men refuse to get off of the rollercoaster. Study these five things carefully and do not let them keep you from transforming your life.

The first thing that keeps men from participating in this process is fear. I know that sounds simple, but it is the foundation of all resistance. If you have ever wondered what is keeping you from reaching your full potential, I can assure you that fear is always at the core of it. Most of us as men believe that fear is a bad thing. Therefore, we deny it and repress it by simply pretending it does not exist. Unfortunately, too many men become paralyzed by their fear and then find creative ways to deny that they are even afraid. This denial keeps them from taking action at an unconscious level. The secret is to simply feel the fear and do it anyway.

The second thing that keeps men from transforming their lives is emotional pain. Unfortunately, most of us do not even recognize that we are in emotional pain because we have been socially conditioned not to truly feel our emotions. In order to avoid feeling our pain, we anesthetize ourselves with things like drugs, work, sex, and alcohol to try to minimize the pain or not feel it at all. This is why so many of us are trapped in denial. We refuse to allow ourselves the opportunity to feel what's really going on in our hearts. It's important to understand that just because we don't feel something does not mean that it does not hurt or is not causing some type of emotional damage. It is this unconscious pain that causes so much dysfunction in our lives. Most of the pain we have is the result of unresolved emotional conflict from our past. Some of this pain is the result of our childhood, while some of it is simply the result of living as a man in today's society.

Chapter 3 ~ The Awakened Male

The third thing that keeps men from transforming their lives is the fear of being perceived as weak. Most men will do anything to maintain their image of being tough, strong, and in control. This is probably the greatest detriment to a man's well-being. This is the reason it is so difficult for men to ask for help. They simply are too afraid of what other people think and how they are perceived as men.

The forth thing that keeps men from transforming their lives is their need to be right. Most men would rather be right than happy. Men are notorious for taking firm positions against things, and they would rather give their lives defending these positions than change them or simply admit that they are wrong. This very rigid need to be right will always keep men from being transformed. In addition to needing to be right, most men also struggle with simply saying, "I don't know." Somehow men have concluded that they are supposed to know everything (which is impossible) and they will do anything to try to project this image of being a know-it-all.

The fifth thing that keeps men from transforming their lives is their inability to see the benefit of emotional and spiritual transformation. As men, we generally process things on an intellectual level. For example, if I tell you that I can show you how to make a million dollars by taking a course in real estate, it's easy for a man to see the benefit of taking that course. In his intellect, he is able to make the connection between taking the course and making a million dollars. On the other hand, if I tell a man that he will experience joy, serenity and inner peace as a result of taking a transformational course, it's difficult, if not impossible, for him to understand that benefit. The reason is the benefit cannot be grasped by the intellect. It can only be experienced in the heart. Most men are so disconnected from their hearts that they cannot see the benefit of experiencing emotional and spiritual transformation.

These are the five things that keep men from transforming their lives. Did you relate to any of them? Which one did you identify with the most? Are you willing to move past these issues and be transformed? I'd like to share some things you can do to help you move through these five obstacles to your transformation.

You must recognize and accept the fact that fear is neither good nor bad, right nor wrong. Fear is simply an emotion that is designed to keep you safe. It is an asset to your well-being, not a liability. Your goal should be to learn to recognize your fears so that you can gain the courage to move through them. The only way out of fear is directly through it, so you must not deny its existence. Learning to recognize and, most importantly, express your fears is a sign of strength, not a sign of weakness. You must learn to connect to your emotions. Learning to feel and express those feelings is probably the most important part of your transformation. Becoming aware of your basic human emotions (I'll discuss these in detail in a moment) is essential to creating and maintaining a rewarding and fulfilling life. Becoming aware of the sources of your pain gives you the impetus to remove that pain. What you can feel you can heal.

Transforming your life is definitely not a weakness. It will take every ounce of your courage and strength to engage in this process. You do not have to be tough and detached to be a man. Although some men may judge and criticize you for taking on this challenge, I can assure you that the rewards and benefits you will receive from your

Chapter 3 ~ The Awakened Male

participation will be priceless. But you must accept the fact that you cannot do it alone. You must be willing to seek support in whatever form you need.

You must be willing to relinquish the need to be right. Letting go of your attachment to being right is essential for your transformation. It is perhaps your greatest challenge. It falls into that category of "simple but not easy." Letting go and surrendering is not the same as giving up and giving in. In addition to this, you must also be willing to simply say, "I don't know." It's okay not to know everything. It does not make you less of a man by saying you don't know something.

There is no way I can put into words the benefit of getting off of the rollercoaster. Words do not come close to the joy and gratitude that I feel on a daily basis as a result of my own transformation. So I'm simply going to ask you to trust me. Trust me that you too can experience joy, gratitude and inner peace. It is already in you. You simply have to commit to your transformation and let it all out.

So are you ready to be transformed? Are you ready, willing and able to engage in the process? As always, the choice is up to you. What will you choose?

I would now like to share what I believe to be the three steps to permanent everlasting transformation. I have come to this conclusion as a result of my own 25 year process. I have personal, first-hand knowledge that these steps work because I have lived them, not just studied and formed theories about them. My knowledge comes from my experience, and that is exactly what I am sharing with you: my own experience. So as you read this, just listen with an open heart and an open mind and see if any of it resonates with you. Try not to judge or criticize what you read, simply ask yourself if it is applicable to you and your life. If so, simply follow the advice given. If not, simply move on to something else.

Step 1

The first step to permanent transformation is to heal your heart. I know that most men will reject this notion but, based on my experience, it is the foundation of personal transformation. Healing our heart means that we learn to connect with and express our feelings. There are basically four primary feelings that we have as human beings. They are, mad, sad, glad, and afraid. These feelings are the language of our souls. They are your internal guidance systems that help you navigate through life. Every other feeling you have is actually just a derivative of or a combination of one or more of these four feelings. For example, when a person says they feel jealous, what it actually means is that they are feeling mad, sad, afraid or a combination of the three. Here is an example: Let's say you see your wife talking to another man. Some men would say that they feel jealous. But if they were willing to look a little deeper, they might come to the awareness that when they see their wife with another man, they possibly feel the energy of anger combined with the energy of sadness. The anger may come as a result of perceived betrayal, while the sadness may be a result of the possibility of losing someone you care about. The point is that the initial energy felt in the body is one or more of the four primary emotions. Emotions are simply energy in motion. There is no energy in the body called "jealous." Jealous is actually a thought that triggers one or more of the primary feelings.

Chapter 3 ~ The Awakened Male

The reason healing your heart is so important is that it teaches you to recognize and make distinctions about your emotions. It also helps you release any pain or hurt from the past that may be sabotaging your current relationships. Although you may not be aware of it, if you have unresolved emotional conflict, it will keep you from truly experiencing who you really are and it will make it extremely difficult to create and maintain healthy fulfilling relationships.

Here is another way to look at it. Have you ever noticed how a child is able to feel and express emotions effortlessly? If a child feels joy, he laughs and smiles. If he feels sadness, he will cry. Kids don't think about emotions; they simply feel them and express them. They intuitively know how to express the energy that is moving through them. What's important to recognize about this is how a child feels emotions and then expresses them and then simply lets go of that emotion. They do not hold onto emotional energy; they allow it to flow through them. A child can be extremely angry at a friend and throw a temper tantrum in one moment, and in the next moment they are happy and joyful and hugging without any residual effects of the emotion of anger. This is how we are supposed to express our feelings. Unfortunately, as men, we are conditioned from a very young age to disconnect from our emotions. Through family and societal conditioning, we learn to start repressing and denying our feelings, which sets us up for emotional disconnection. Eventually we lose the ability to feel and we then begin processing everything through our intellect. In my opinion, this is the source of all of our addictive behaviors. When a man loses the ability to connect to his emotions, he begins to over analyze and stay stuck in his head. His unresolved emotional conflict causes him to "think" instead of feel and that is the source of a lot of his pain and suffering.

I believe this is why so many relationships fail: as men, we do not know how to connect to our hearts and express our very basic emotional needs. This disconnection keeps us from truly being "relational" in our relationships and that is why they fail.

Think of your heart as a balloon. Every time you feel an emotion, the balloon fills up with air. When you allow yourself to simply feel the emotion and then express that emotion, it's like exhaling the air from the balloon. If you are emotionally healthy, you are able to feel the emotion (fill the balloon) and then express your feelings appropriately (release the air). This inhaling and exhaling keeps the heart healthy and functioning properly. But, if every time you feel an emotion you keep it bottled up inside of you without releasing it, your heart begins to build up pressure. Eventually the pressure becomes so great that something has to happen so the balloon pops. This popping of the balloon causes men to act out in violent and inappropriate ways.

Think of why some men act out so violently during road rage. Do you really believe that the person is really angry simply because they were cut off on the highway? I believe the reason some men act out this way is because they have all of this pent-up anger and sadness inside of them and they do not know how to release it. So when they encounter someone who they perceive to be the source of their anger, they simply lash out in the way that they are accustomed to. Their balloon pops, and it is expressed through senseless acts of violence.

This is not only expressed through road rage. Whenever you see stories of domestic violence or child abuse, the same principle applies. A man has not been taught to heal his heart and he is walking around with all of this pent-up, negative energy. The only way he knows how to deal with it is through striking out with violence. By teaching a man to heal his heart, we can minimize or eliminate these violent acts. When our country accepts this fact, I can assure you that we will begin seeing a reduction in our prison population and an overall reduction in senseless acts of violence. But in order to do this, we must help men get off of the societal rollercoaster. We must encourage men to heal their hurts so that they will stop hurting each other. By engaging them in their emotional transformation, we lay the foundation for the eradication of a large percentage of the social ills that currently plague our world.

Emotional healing is the process one must go through if they are truly committed to their transformation. You must understand that there is a distinction between motivation and transformation. Motivation is usually temporary, while transformation is permanent. If you commit to your emotional healing, I can promise you that your transformation will stay with you the rest of your life. Heal your heart, transform your life!

Step 2

The next step to getting off of the rollercoaster is the constant expansion of your mind and intellect. Although most people who go to college tend to stop learning once they graduate, I believe that learning is a lifelong process that each of us must engage in. If you are truly committed to your transformation, you must recognize that your mind is like a muscle. It simply gets stronger the more you use it. Make sure you exercise this muscle by reading books, participating in seminars, listening to intellectually stimulating programs, and taking courses to learn new things. Studies have shown that people who engage their minds on a regular basis are far less likely to develop Alzheimer's disease in their later years.

Expanding your mind and intellect also means challenging your long-held beliefs and points of view. If you've never interacted with someone of a different race, now would be a good time to take that on. If you're the type of person who sees the glass as half empty, find an optimist who sees the glass as half full and engage in some dialog with him. Listen with an open mind, and challenge yourself to see things from a different point of view. Most importantly, make sure that you commit to discovering who you really are. This is an inside job and it is the most important decision you will ever make. Discovering who you really are is the reason you are here. It is your sole responsibility as a human being. If you are successful in this endeavor, I can assure you that everything else will pale in comparison. Discovering who you really are is the Holy Grail of your existence. Be sure to make it your priority by expanding your mind and challenging your intellect.

Step 3

The third step to permanent transformation is to develop a spiritual connection with something greater than yourself. As a former atheist, I completely understand if you are skeptical about this step. On the other hand, I also know there are those of you who completely agree with me. The fact of the matter is that you must find your own truth when it comes to spirituality. When I say, "Develop a spiritual connection," I am not asking you to accept any religious dogma or doctrine. I'm not asking you to go to church or to be "converted." I'm simply asking you to be open minded to the possibility that there is a power greater than yourself in the universe. Some people call this power God, Yahweh, Jehovah, Great Spirit, Jesus, Buddha, Krishna or Mohammed. I do not believe that the name that you use is that important. I do, however, believe that it is of the utmost importance that you develop a relationship with it no matter what name you use.

So there you have it. The three steps to permanent transformation:

> Step 1. Heal your heart.
>
> Step 2. Expand your mind and intellect.
>
> Step 3. Develop a spiritual connection with something greater than yourself.

I would now like to share some steps I've taken to assist me in engaging and maintaining my personal transformation. I want you to understand that the things I am about to share have worked for me. There is no guarantee that they will work for you. As always, trust your own inner wisdom as you read my suggestions. Each human being is unique. You must accept your uniqueness and be willing to act on any impulse that you feel. If it feels right to you, heed the suggestions.

Healing My Heart

As I've mentioned, I have spent the last twenty years fully engaged in my own transformation. If I were to choose the one thing that had the most impact on healing my heart it would have to be inner-child work. Inner-child work allowed me to get to the source of my pain and the foundation of all of my negative behaviors. Inner-child work helped me to recognize how my abusive childhood was still affecting my behavior some thirty years later. There are some people who believe that it isn't necessary to "dig up" old wounds to be transformed, but in my case, it was the one thing that really helped me heal my heart. Uncovering the hidden hurts released me from their unconscious grip. Inner-child work was the process that set my heart free. The amazing thing about inner-child work was that it helped me recognize the "why" of my behavior. Although I was always highly motivated and ambitious, this work taught me the true reasons behind my motivation. All of the motivational seminars I attended prior to my participation simply fueled my deep feelings of inadequacy. I learned I was always motivated because I had this insatiable need to gain other people's approval. By recognizing this fact, I was able to learn to love myself regardless of any of my accomplishments. Once I let go of my need to impress other people, I freed myself to be as motivated as I wanted to be. With my new understanding I was motivated in an authentic way. This is the truth that set me free.

Through the process of inner-child work, I reconnected with my emotions and it has brought me joy and peace beyond description.

Another important piece of healing my heart was journaling. I began journaling as a result of my experience with a therapist. Journaling is an amazing process and one of the most effective ways of healing your heart. It allows you to access deep-rooted feelings and beliefs about yourself that may be the cause of the pain and suffering in your life. Learning to journal not only helped me discover who I am, it also uncovered the hidden writer inside of me that I did not know existed.

Chapter 3 ~ The Awakened Male

Expanding My Mind

Without question, my saving grace has been my love and passion for learning. From a very early age, I have always loved reading and learning new things. With all of today's technology, there is absolutely no reason for a person not to engage in expanding their mind. The Internet is an inexhaustible resource of information, which provides the perfect vehicle for expanding your mind and intellect. I personally love the Internet and technology because it gives me access to any information I need on any subject. With access to this information, I can always learn new things and expand my mind.

I also commit to reading a minimum of five new books a year. Although I probably average a lot more than this, I make sure that I read at least five. I believe that reading is for the mind what exercise is for the body. This is my exercise for my brain and it keeps my intellect sharp and my decision-making skills at their best.

Another great resource for expanding my mind is seminars. I must admit that I am a self-confessed seminar junkie. I love intellectually stimulating conversations and learning from some of the world's great minds. Seminars give me the exposure to new ways of thinking and perceiving the world and they challenge me to get out of my comfort zone and see things from a new and different perspective. What's wonderful about the Internet and technology is that I can attend seminars in the comfort of my own home on my computer without having to interact with anyone personally. But whenever I feel the need to engage face to face with like-minded people, I simply participate in a seminar or workshop that fulfills my need to interact and learn with others.

There is absolutely no excuse for people not to expand their minds and learn new things. The only thing that can prevent people from doing this is themselves.

Developing My Spiritual Connection

First and foremost, I had to come to my own truth about God. I had to become willing to admit that there was a power greater than myself in the universe. After I was able to accept this truth, I had to develop my own spiritual practices to insure that I deepen my relationship with this power.

Here are three things that I do that help me deepen my spiritual connection.

Prayer

Prayer to me is simply having an ongoing dialog with my Creator. By communicating with my source, I develop a deep level of intimacy and connection to that which is greater than myself. This prayer takes many forms. It can be reading a spiritual message or listening to a spiritual messenger and then engaging in a conversation about what I heard, or it can mean having an attitude of gratitude for being alive. Prayer to me is simply concentrated thought. As long as I'm thinking about that which is greater than myself, I am actually engaged in prayer.

Meditation

One thing I learned as a result of my transformation was the importance of meditation. Meditation is one of the greatest gifts that I have ever given myself. Meditation is my way of staying connected to my source, and it calms my spirit and eases my mind. It is only through the process of meditation that I was able to learn to quiet my mind so I could learn to listen to that still, small voice of wisdom within me. It is an extremely important aspect of my transformation, and it is something that I wholeheartedly recommend that you consider doing for yourself.

Contemplation

Contemplation is the process of thinking intently about God. To assist me in this process, I subscribe to several different spiritual resources that send me daily spiritual e-mails. As I read the e-mails and contemplate their messages, it deepens my awareness and understanding of God. By being willing to engage in this deep contemplation, I come to my own truth and understanding about God and it puts my heart at ease.

There you have them: prayer, meditation and contemplation, the three keys to deepening your spiritual connection.

These are some things that I do to keep my transformation permanently imbedded in my heart, mind and spirit. If any of these feel right to you, check them out and participate. I believe that if you truly set an intention to get off of the rollercoaster, you will be divinely guided to the perfect people and experiences to assist you in the process. Always remember the three steps to permanent transformation. Make a commitment to these three steps and your life will be transformed for the better.

> Step 1. Heal your heart.
>
> Step 2. Expand your mind and intellect.

Step 3. Develop a spiritual connection with something greater than yourself.

If you will commit to following the advice from this chapter, I can assure you that you will get off of the rollercoaster. Another way of looking at this is that you become an awakened male who is no longer following society's rules but who is able to listen to and trust his own heart which will guide him to becoming an authentic male.

You can do this!

A tribe is a group of people connected to one another, connected to a leader, and connected to an idea. For millions of years, human beings have been part of one tribe or another. A group needs only two things to be a tribe: a shared interest and a way to communicate.

Seth Godin

Chapter 4
What Is A Men's Group?

A couple of years ago, I received an invitation through social media to join an online group for men called The Virtual Men's Gathering. I was quite familiar with participating in live men's groups and their structure and I was intrigued by the potential of finding out just how effective a virtual men's group could actually be so I accepted the invitation and became a member.

It just so happened that I knew two of the men personally who had also agreed to join the group. We had met at a workshop a couple of years prior and I felt really comfortable being in the group with them.

Before I share my experience of participating in the virtual group I would like to share an article by a man named Jayson Gaddis who is a therapist and men's coach who I really respect and admire.

You may not have had any exposure to men's work or men's groups so I would like to share his article to give you some insights on what a men's group is.

This article is being reprinted with his permission.

Since 1991, I have been in men-only groups in a variety of settings. In college I lived with 17 men for three years. I then worked for my fraternity for two years traveling the country facilitating conversation and leadership workshops with only men.

For the past eleven years, I have led wilderness rite-of-passage trips with [boys](#) and men. I have even led leadership workshops at fraternity conventions with 1000+ men. I have spent thousands of hours with just men in a variety of settings. But nothing quite compares to what happens when 8-12 guys sit in a circle and get real.

I have been in a men's group for the past five years and these guys have witnessed me in all my colors. They have supported me and challenged me through two breakups, marriage, fathering a kid, building a business and much more.

From 2009-2011, I led a six-month men's group called the [Men's Leadership Training](#) to see what is possible when a small group of men collaborate and really work on themselves toward a greater purpose.

What about you? When was the last time you got real with another man and showed yourself to him? When was the last time another man called you on your bullshit? When was the last time you sobbed in front of another man?

Purpose & Value of a Men's Group

In my view, the purpose of any men's group is multi-faceted. Likewise, the value is not only very subjective, it runs many layers deep. Try joining one and see what value you receive.

In a nutshell, men's groups are about getting four things in your life: Clarity, Accountability, Challenge, and Support.

Chapter 4 ~ What Is A Men's Group?

I have recently pinpointed what I call the nine P's in men's personal development that are essential for a man to know and learn if he is to grow and evolve. And, the nine P's apply to men's groups.

The Nine P's

Partnership. This is the biggest "P" of all. This is about relationship. Ever heard of a business partner? An accountability partner at the gym? A partner for life? Like it or not, a men's group is a committed partnership. Even if you don't like a guy in your men's group, you get to practice being in partnership, in relationship, with him. You are there to hold each other accountable to what you say you will do. When you join a men's group, you make a commitment to the men in your group to stay in the fire of the relationship without bailing out. For most guys, when things get hard, they just leave. For guys in a serious men's group, they get in the ring and stay in the ring. When it's time to leave, it gets talked about directly.

Power. Most men just don't have access to their full conscious power as a man. Men's groups help you get in touch with your full power– express it, share it and be witnessed in it.

Purpose. A common thread in a men's group is the common purpose which we are discussing here. But within the context of the group purpose is each individual purpose. Do you know why you are on the planet? What is your life's purpose? A men's group can help you explore this.

Presence. A men's group without presence is a big fat waste of time. It's just another intellectual discussion about concepts. When men learn to become present with their experience in the moment, they are more likely to feel and more likely to be congruent. In a men's group, you learn tools to help you "get present."

Principled. Essentially, this means integrity. You do what you say you will do because you know your values and where you stand. You know yourself well enough to have principles. However, contrary to a lot of men, these are constantly evolving to support your evolution as a man.

Practice. Men's groups are all about practice for the real world. Just like a basketball player practices free throws so he is more likely to sink them in the big game, when men practice being authentically themselves, they are more likely to stay authentic and open in the real world. For example, I might practice saying something hard in my men's group to another man, so that I have more confidence to say it to my boss the following day.

In a group of guys in this context, you *practice*:

- congruence–(thoughts, words, & actions all line up)
- being authentic (being who you really are without hiding)
- taking responsibility
- openness, open heartedness (really listening to, and understanding, others)
- feeling your feelings
- speaking your truth & skillful communication (i.e. dealing with conflict)

Prayer. Yup, prayer. I'm not religious, but I am a spiritual dude. Prayer may happen at the beginning or end of a group. It's a shout out to whatever you believe in or to someone you love. Asking for guidance, wisdom for yourself, the men in the circle or sending a prayer to someone you love.

Possibility. Ah yes, what is possible for you and each man in the group? Individually? Collectively?

Play. A group of guys getting together in this way can be very serious. That's why we need to lighten up in every group and have some fun. This can happen before, during or after your group. I'm a serious guy, so play is critical for me to stay open to my smile, to my laughter and to having fun with bros I care about. For example, the men's group I've been in for the past five years just implemented a monthly night to celebrate together and play together.

Why Not Turn To Women For Support?

It is a common experience among men to go to their girlfriends or wives for support, emotional or otherwise. Women get tired of this dynamic. They don't want to be your lover and your mother. Women tell me all the time how they wish their partner had more quality man friends.

Only seeking support from women is a slippery slope. That is why it is critical to get some honest feedback from your fellow men. We need support and wisdom from both sexes if we want to grow as men.

What Men's Groups Are Not:

Don't worry, men's groups are not group therapy, although they can be very therapeutic. Men's groups are not a bunch of guys sitting around a fire singing Kumbaya. Men's groups are not a bunch of weird freaky men just talking about their feelings (although I can be weird and freaky and talk about my feelings).

Men's groups are definitely not for dudes who would rather keep things very much on the surface and who are afraid of intimacy, although a group can help with that guy's fears. Remember, a men's group is for a brave man who is willing to face the music of his own life. There are men's groups all over the world right now, each with their own unique flavor and purpose.

A men's group can be a great support when you are going through a tough time in your life and need help. A men's group can also be a place where you celebrate the victories in your life with great people and explore what is possible in your life.

Ultimately, a men's group will challenge you to be who you are without hesitation, reservation or apology so that you can be the powerful guy you are who is free, fulfilled and full of energy to serve the world.

So, How And Where Do I Start?

~ ~ ~ ~ ~

In its simplest form, a men's group is a group of committed men who come together with the intention of supporting and empowering each other to live rewarding and fulfilling lives. You do not have to have

Chapter 4 ~ What Is A Men's Group?

a degree or any special qualifications to participate. Most men who participate have had some exposure to dealing with their emotional and psychological baggage through seminars, workshops or maybe reading a book that introduced them to the concept of male transformation. But ultimately the only thing that is required is a commitment to learning and growing and being open-minded and open-hearted.

Participating in a men's group challenges men to examine how they show up in life. It's about taking full responsibility for your thoughts feelings and beliefs and being willing to share your inner world with the group. This can be extremely difficult for men because, as I mentioned earlier, current male conditioning has convinced men that it's not okay to talk about their feelings and emotions.

Most men may be comfortable talking about sports, politics, sex, women and making money, but very few men are capable of being open and vulnerable and discussing his fear, his sadness, his pain or his joys.

What makes a men's group unique is how men learn to hold space for each other. Holding space is a sacred and transformational process that truly helps a man grow and heal. To better understand what holding space truly is and how it works, I would like to share some excerpts from a beautifully written article by Heather Plett. You can find more of her amazing work at www.heatherplatt.com

Here are the excerpts from the article:

What does it mean to "hold space" for someone else?

It means that we are willing to walk alongside another person in whatever journey they're on without judging them, making them feel inadequate, trying to fix them or trying to impact the outcome. When we hold space for other people, we open our hearts, offer unconditional support and let go of judgment and control.

Sometimes we find ourselves *holding space* for people while they *hold space* for others. In our situation, for example, Ann was *holding space* for us while we *held space* for Mom. Though I know nothing about her support system, I suspect that there are others *holding space* for Ann as she does this challenging and meaningful work. It's virtually impossible to be a strong space holder unless we have others who will *hold space* for us. Even the strongest leaders, coaches, nurses, etc., need to know that there are some people with whom they can be vulnerable and weak without fear of being judged.

In my own roles as teacher, facilitator, coach, mother, wife, and friend, etc., I do my best to *hold space* for other people in the same way that Ann modeled it for me and my siblings. It's not always easy, because I have a very human tendency to want to fix people, give them advice, or judge them for not being further along the path than they are, but I keep trying because I know that it's important. At the same time, there are people in my life who I trust to *hold space* for me.

To truly support people in their own growth, transformation, grief, etc., we can't do it by taking their power away (i.e. trying to fix their problems), shaming them (i.e. implying that they should know more than they do) or overwhelming them (i.e. giving them more information than they're ready for). We have to be prepared to step to the side so that they can make their own choices, offer them unconditional love and support, give gentle guidance when it's needed, and make them feel safe even when they make mistakes.

Holding space is not something that's exclusive to facilitators, coaches, or palliative care nurses. It is something that ALL of us can do for each other – for our partners, children, friends, neighbors, and even strangers who strike up conversations as we're riding the bus to work.

8 Tips to Help You Hold Space for Others

Here are the lessons I've learned from Ann and others who have held space for me.

1. Give people permission to trust their own intuition and wisdom. When we were supporting Mom in her final days, we had no experience to rely on, and yet, intuitively, we knew what was needed. We knew how to carry her shrinking body to the washroom, we knew how to sit and sing hymns to her, and we knew how to love her. We even knew when it was time to inject the medication that would help ease her pain. In a very gentle way, Ann let us know that we didn't need to do things according to some arbitrary healthcare protocol – we simply needed to trust our intuition and accumulated wisdom from the many years we'd loved Mom.

2. Give people only as much information as they can handle. Ann gave us some simple instructions and left us with a few handouts, but did not overwhelm us with far more than we could process in our tender time of grief. Too much information would have left us feeling incompetent and unworthy.

3. Don't take their power away. When we take decision-making power out of people's hands, we leave them feeling useless and incompetent. There may be some times when we need to step in and make hard decisions for other people (i.e. when they're dealing with an addiction and an intervention feels like the only thing that will save them), but in almost every other case, people need the autonomy to make their own choices (even our children). Ann knew that we needed to feel empowered in making decisions on our Mom's behalf, and so she offered support but never tried to direct or control us.

4. Keep your own ego out of it. This is a big one. We all get caught in that trap now and then – when we begin to believe that someone else's success is dependent on our intervention, or when we think that their failure reflects poorly on us, or when we're convinced that whatever emotions they choose to unload on us are about us instead of them. It's a trap I've occasionally found myself slipping into when I teach. I can become more concerned about my own success (Do the students like me? Do their marks reflect on my ability to teach? etc.) than about the success of my students. But that doesn't serve anyone – not even me. To truly support their growth, I need to keep my ego out of it and create the space where they have the opportunity to grow and learn.

5. Make them feel safe enough to fail. When people are learning, growing, or going through grief or transition, they are bound to make some mistakes along the way. When we, as their space holders, withhold judgment and shame, we offer them the opportunity to reach inside themselves to find the courage to take risks and the resilience to keep going even when they fail. When we let them know that failure is simply a part of the journey and not the end of the world, they'll spend less time beating themselves up for it and more time learning from their mistakes.

6. Give guidance and help with humility and thoughtfulness. A wise space holder knows when to withhold guidance (i.e. when it makes a person feel foolish and inadequate) and when to offer it gently (i.e. when a person asks for it or is too lost to know what to ask for). Though Ann did not take our power or autonomy away, she did offer to come and give Mom baths and do some of the more challenging parts of care giving. This was a relief to us, as we had no practice at it and didn't want to place Mom in a position that might make her feel shame (i.e. having her children see her naked). This is a careful dance that we all must do when we hold space for other people. Recognizing the areas in which they feel most vulnerable and incapable and offering the right kind of help without shaming them takes practice and humility.

7. Create a container for complex emotions, fear, trauma, etc. When people feel that they are held in a deeper way than they are used to, they feel safe enough to allow complex emotions to surface that might normally remain hidden. Someone who is practiced at *holding space* knows that this can happen and will be prepared to hold it in a gentle, supportive, and non-judgmental way. In The Circle Way, we talk about "holding the rim" for people.

The circle becomes the space where people feel safe enough to fall apart without fearing that this will leave them permanently broken or that they will be shamed by others in the room. Someone is always there to offer strength and courage. This is not easy work, and it is work that I continue to learn about as I host increasingly more challenging conversations. We cannot do it if we are overly emotional ourselves, if we haven't done the hard work of looking into our own shadow, or if we don't trust the people we are holding space for. In Ann's case, she did this by showing up with tenderness, compassion and confidence. If she had shown up in a way that didn't offer us assurance that she could handle difficult situations or that she was afraid of death, we wouldn't have been able to trust her as we did.

8. Allow them to make different decisions and to have different experiences than you would. Holding space is about respecting each person's differences and recognizing that those differences may lead to them making choices that we would not make. Sometimes, for example, they make choices based on cultural norms that we can't understand from within our own experience. When we hold space, we release control and we honor differences. This showed up, for example, in the way that Ann supported us in making decisions about what to do with Mom's body after her spirit was no longer housed there. If there had been some ritual that we felt we needed to conduct before releasing her body, we were free to do that in the privacy of Mom's home.

Holding space is not something that we can master overnight, or that can be adequately addressed in a list of tips like the ones I've just offered. It's a complex practice that evolves as we practice it, and it is unique to each person and each situation.

Chapter 4 ~ What Is A Men's Group?

~ ~ ~ ~ ~

Holding space is the beauty and power that comes from a men's group. It takes lots of courage, vulnerability, sensitivity and patience but the payoff is worth the effort. Unfortunately, most men are too afraid to expose themselves at this emotional level but my experience has taught me that it is the only way to truly break free from the emotional and psychological scars that might be holding us back.

When I joined the Virtual Men's Gathering, I had had plenty of exposure of being in men's groups already. Because of my own growth, I had no problems sharing my thoughts and feelings with other men and I was very comfortable "holding space" for others. My real question was whether or not a virtual online meeting would help facilitate more growth for me and could we also hold space within a virtual environment.

I must admit that I was pleasantly surprised with the diversity of our online group. Men were from the Czech Republic, Canada, Norway, Spain, USA and Portugal. They ranged from age 21 to late 60's and were single, married and divorced. What we all had in common was a willingness to be authentic and share openly and honestly with each other and that is what makes it effective.

The amazing thing about today's technology is that it allows you to communicate with almost anyone anywhere in the world. Using online software, we were able to meet online and see and communicate with each other through video and audio. We were definitely able to hold space for each other and create intimate connections despite the miles between us.

After participating in this group for over a year, I can attest that virtual men's groups are effective and efficient. Although I prefer face-to-face contact and being in live groups, an online group can definitely facilitate emotional healing and growth. All that is needed is a group of men to come together with the intention of building an online support network that "holds space" and encourages each man to speak his truth and be fully present in the group.

So if you've been thinking about starting a group, or maybe participating in one, rest assured that there are lots of options available to you. You are no longer limited by age, location education level, socio-economic status, religion or sexual orientation. If you truly want to experience the magic of men's groups, simply make a commitment to yourself to find one and then take Nike's advice and just do it!

I can assure you that joining a men's group can be the most powerful and transformational experiences of a man's life. If you're ready to move past superficial conversations and relationships and are ready for a deeper experience of being a man and experiencing life, a men's group could be exactly what you're looking for.

If you're truly ready to change your life and join a group, I will be providing some tips on starting/joining a men's group in an upcoming chapter.

What the society thinks is of no interest to me. All that's important is how I see myself. I know who I am. I know the value of my work.

Robin S. Sharma

Chapter 5
What Are The Benefits Of Men's Work?

I'm often asked why should men participate in men's work and my simple answer is because it will support you in becoming genuinely happy with your life. I believe for most men this applies. As simplistic as it may sound, I believe this is what all men really want, though most of us don't truly know how to get it.

Doing men's work is invaluable because it supports men in developing authentic connected friendships and relationships with other men. It also positively affects our relationships with women, both personally and professionally. It supports men in becoming better husbands and fathers. It empowers men to be more productive in their professional lives and it provides men with a deep feeling of inner peace and connectedness. It connects men to their hearts and souls and allows for vulnerability and intimacy, which leads to connection and belonging. When men experience this, it automatically begins eradicating a lot of the social ills that plague our world because a happy man is a non-violent man and a happy man is a loving man.

In order to look into some of the benefits of men's work, I would like to share a transcript of an interview I did on my radio show. My show is titled 'A New Conversation With Men' and it is based on my book of the same title. The intention of the show is to interview men and women who are committed to improving the lives of men by supporting a new paradigm of masculinity that propels men to live extraordinary lives.

In the interview, I'm speaking with Terry Hartwick about a program called the New Warrior Training Adventure and he and I are sharing our insights from participating in this remarkable program created specifically to empower men to embrace a new paradigm of masculinity. Our conversation really encapsulates a lot of the benefits of doing men's work whether you participate in the New Warrior Training or not.

It is a verbatim transcript of our interview so it will be written in that format. The title of the interview is 'The New Warrior Training Adventure' and it was broadcast on March 11th 2016

Show Intro:

The time has come for a new revolution, not a revolution of violence or control, but a revolution of the mind, the heart and the soul. A revolution that will touch the heart of men and let them know that they no longer have to pretend. This is a place where men get to be real, because in this space they can say exactly what they feel. So men of all races unite and come in. This journey will challenge you to look deep within. So, let the new revolution begin because it's time for a new conversation with men.

Michael:

Welcome to new conversation with men, where my intention is to

Chapter 5 ~ What Are The Benefits Of Men's Work?

educate, motivate and inspire men to reach their full potential and live extraordinary lives, I'm your host, Coach Michael Taylor. I'd like for you take a moment and think about this question, really give it some thought. Are you ready? What is the greatest challenge facing the world today? Obviously that is a really big question, because there are definitely lots of challenges out there. But, based on your own beliefs about the world, what do you think is the greatest challenge? Here are just a few challenges facing our world, so let's see if any of these made your list. How about racism? Currently in America we are faced with lots of challenges surrounding race. It isn't just an American problem, so I will list it as one of the big challenges facing the world.

What about nuclear war? I recently read that North Korea was testing nuclear weapons. This could definitely be considered as a big challenge facing the world. Then, there's poverty and corporate greed and political corruption. There's climate change and global warming, there's violence, and mass killings, and the list goes on and on.

So which is the greatest challenge? I'm not sure that I could actually pick just one. Each of these problems presents a unique challenge that we will ultimately have to resolve if we want to create a better world for future generations. Though I can't pick just one, I will say that one of the greatest challenges we have wasn't even on the list that I just read. In my opinion, if we solve this one challenge, the majority of the other challenges will automatically disappear.

What is this challenge? I believe the challenge is to redefine manhood and create a new paradigm of masculinity. By doing so, I believe we will begin to see the eradication of the majority of the social ills that currently plague our world. When I say this, some people will argue that I'm male bashing and saying that men are responsible for most of the world's problems. Nothing could be further from the truth. What I'm suggesting is that we currently have a male culture that needs to be transformed and the only way to do this is to engage men in a new conversation about manhood and masculinity.

The more men we engage in this conversation, the more we change the culture, and when we change the culture, we fix the problem. I'm reminded of the famous quote by Albert Einstein, who so wonderfully stated, "All the problems of a society cannot be resolved with the same level of thinking that created them in the first place." In order to change the culture, we must begin by changing our thinking about that culture, and when we do that, the culture will change. That is why I named this show, "a new conversation with men." My intention is to engage men and women in a dialogue about ways we can work together to shift the male culture of the planet. It isn't about attacking or condemning, it is about supporting and empowering men to embrace new ways of being and relating as men.

It's about creating that new level of thinking Albert Einstein was talking about. Fortunately, a movement has been growing over the past 30 years or so called the men's movement and I believe it's one of the most important movements that the world has ever seen. Since this movement began, more and more men are recognizing that the roles of masculinity are changing rapidly and men must be willing to embrace these changing roles if they truly want to live extraordinary lives.

Chapter 5 ~ What Are The Benefits Of Men's Work?

One organization that has deeply impacted this movement is The Mankind project. They offer an amazing three day workshop that was specifically designed to challenge men to examine how society and culture shape our beliefs about masculinity. They also provide a wide variety of other programs that support men in shifting some antiquated ideas and beliefs about manhood, about sexism, about racism, and a host of other societal challenges. Their primary workshop is called The New Warrior Training Adventure, and it is appropriately titled because deep down inside all men truly are warriors. Unfortunately, most men have not had the training and support to be authentic warriors and therefore, too many of them lose their way due to the current masculine culture that I mentioned.

Tonight, we're going to be talking about The New Warrior Training Adventure. As a graduate of the program, I can attest that it was one of the most powerful and transformational experiences of my life, and, as a matter of fact, it's one of the reasons that I started this show. As a direct result of the training, I made a commitment that I would do something that would support men in waking up and stop living lives of quiet desperation, and that's how and why a new conversation with men was born.

I have a graduate who is going to be sharing his experience of participating in the training. My hope is that our conversation will pique an interest in you to consider going on the adventure yourself. If you feel moved, we will be providing contact information at the end of the show.

Let me begin by introducing our guest. Actually I'd like to give our guest an opportunity to introduce himself, and he will do this in a way that the new warrior training teaches us. It's called the check in. So, let's have our guest check in right now. Let's see, Terry Hartwick would you check in please?

Terry:

Yes, thank you Michael. I'm checking in at this time and this moment, I have a lot of joy in my life just for where I'm at as far as my relationships with my partner and my family. Most important right now is that I'm extremely excited to be able to share the work I've been doing that has changed my life, so I'm in lots of joy.

Michael:

I'm going to be checking in with that same joy. I'm really excited to have you on the show. I've got a couple of other men who hopefully will show up and we'll give them a place to check in once they do show up, but if they don't, you and I, I'm sure, will have a wonderful conversation in sharing this warrior training work. I'm feeling that joy, I know it's infectious because I know that when we do this work, we really commit to transforming our lives. There's a part of us that sort of wakes up, and we're filled with this aliveness and this passion for living and so that's what I'm checking in with right now. I'm checking in with this joy and this passion for being alive and doing what I love to do, which is radio. I love doing radio. It is one of my passions so that's what I'm checking in with.

Terry, let's do this, let's begin with this. It's my belief that there are only two things that would cause a man to want to change: the number one reason is pain, and the other reason is what I call divine discontent. It's that internal feeling we have inside of us that something just isn't right and most of the time, we have no idea where the feeling comes from or what we should do about it. I'd like to know how you first became involved with men's work in general. Was it pain, or was it that divine discontent?

Terry:

I'm aware, Michael, that we haven't really talked and discussed this beforehand so when you say pain, yes. I have a unique disease, where my repressed emotions cause physical pain. It was discovered by a doctor many years ago. It's been documented and there'll be a documentary coming out shortly by John Sarno I experienced pain from burying my emotions, which actually cause physical pain in my body, which is a psychosomatic condition.

Michael:

That's something I think society as a whole is beginning to recognize: how repressed emotions can definitely have a physical effect on our body. From my perspective, my pain was a little different. This is how I actually became involved with men's work. I had gone through a divorce, a bankruptcy, a foreclosure, basically lost everything. There I was, bankrupt, depressed and all alone and at the time, I didn't recognize it as pain, I just recognized it as challenges that I needed to try to figure out how to fix, and that was one of the problems. I was so disconnected from my emotions that I didn't feel the pain, I didn't understand what the depression even was. It took me a while to get to this place where I began to recognize that something had to change. My pain was so great that I personally had to make a choice, and that choice was to either get help or die - there was no in between. Fortunately for me, I didn't drink, or do drugs or alcohol or I'm sure I probably wouldn't be doing this show right now because I probably would be dead. I really believe that, but fortunately for me, the pain got so great that I knew that I had to do something. I gained the courage to initially go to therapy, and it was that courage, it was that choice that really put me on the journey of transformation and at the time I knew absolutely nothing about men's work. I just knew that I needed to alleviate the pain that I was in, and I needed to do something to change my life. I gained the courage to go to therapy that put me on the path of what we call transformation. With that said, Terry, how were you actually introduced to the new warrior training?

Terry:

It's interesting because I had no idea that the physical pain I had was connected to the repressed emotions. It took me 13 years. I had major surgeries, back surgeries, shoulder surgeries, all in an effort to cut out the pain and it was amazing how many surgeons I found who were willing to do it. It wasn't until after 13 years of endless surgeries and pain that I came across a doctor who actually had done work in this. The process is called TMS, Tension Myositis Syndrome, and he actually identified it and brought to my attention that it's possible that your physical pain is related to repressed emotions.

It turned out he was a warrior brother who had been introduced to the warrior training. It didn't have anything to do with the symptoms I had but he was a medical doctor and suggested that quite possibly getting in touch with my emotions might help with my physical pain. I never would have thought of it, never would have dreamed of it, but I was pretty much at my wit's end, exasperated and physically just not even able to function anymore with my back pain, lying in bed. I was basically dying in my mind and it wasn't until I had this concept that I realized it was quite possibly from my repressed emotions. I tried it, I experimented with it, I opened up, I started doing some lessons with it, and in a matter eight to nine months, my pain level had dropped 80% and after that I was in full recovery.

Michael:

Wow, what a story.

Terry:

Yeah, and so I was to go say it's pretty bizarre, for the individuals that aren't aware of psycho traumatic conditions about how your body can cause physical pain. It's hard to believe but it has been going on since man evolved. It's just a simple thing like when the individual blushes, their skin temperature changes. When you're in fear, you perspire, it's all relative, it's all a psychosomatic emission. It's the power of the unconscious mind which drives a lot of our lives and in my case as well.

Michael:

What's really powerful about that is, as men, we are taught and conditioned at a very early age that it's not okay to feel, it's not okay to express our emotions. In one of my books, which is clearly what this radio show is based upon called, "A New Conversation with Men," I talk about what I call the five illusions of manhood. The first primary illusion is that, to be a man, we must be non-emotional and disconnected. I would assert that the overwhelming majority of pain that we have in our lives, whether we recognize it or not, is because of that illusion. It's that we are taught and conditioned that it's not okay for us to feel, and we live in a society and culture that says they want to cut you open, they want to give you drugs, they want to do all these things to try to fix you, but none of them actually gets to the cause of the pain, which I believe, as you said it, that the emotional experiences that we're holding onto literally has a physical effect on our body. It isn't until we as men, become open minded enough to recognize that as human beings, we have emotions for a reason and if we don't know how to express them appropriately then they will cause physical ailments in our body.

I believe that's why this work that we're going to be talking about tonight is so, so very important because it's one of the few resources that I'm aware of that was created to give men a space to deal with, address with, get in touch with all aspects of their humanity, especially their emotions. It creates that safe space where men can come together and really get real and honest with each other. When we do that, I know without question we can begin healing in lots and lots of different ways; emotionally, psychologically, and spiritually. Terry, I want you to think about this. You talked about the physical pain, and all of that that was driving a lot of your behavior, but before the training, if you can put that physical ailment aside and try to remember Terry before he actually did the warrior training, aside from the physical challenges, can

Chapter 5 ~ What Are The Benefits Of Men's Work?

you describe yourself before you actually went through the training.

Terry:

Well, I remember that as if it was yesterday because it was my life. Unfortunately, I didn't start this training until I was 55 years old. Terry before the training was full of rage because he was taught not to feel. He was raised in an environment where he wasn't treated properly as an individual. He did not have a map on how to behave as being an accountable, respectable individual. All I had was, the father who taught me, and basically was experiencing a lot of anger. The behavior that I had was anger, very defensive, not owning my emotions, throwing my emotions out on other people and I was extremely defensive and full of rage.

Michael:

Amazingly, I was the flip side of that coin. Before the training, I was the people pleasing nice guy and I really didn't know how to express anger appropriately. I didn't allow myself to express anger because in my mind that was bad, that I wasn't supposed to be angry, I wasn't supposed to experience and express anger. I completely repressed and suppressed all anger. What that did was drive a co-dependent behavior, in which I was always trying to get other people's approval because I was too afraid to be authentic in what was really going on inside of me. I had to literally relearn how to feel and express anger.

Interestingly enough, one of the ways that I was able to do that, what kind of drove me in that direction is, I read an interesting book by a woman named Louise Hay. The book was titled, "You Can Heal

Your Life." It's about how certain ailments could be traced back to emotional blocks. In her book she said that people who struggled with expressing anger will generally have lots of throat problems. When I read that, a light bulb just went off in my head because I recognized that all my life I had been troubled with things like tonsillitis and sore throats and all of that and I immediately was able to connect the fact that I didn't know how to express anger appropriately to those physical ailments in my throat. I had been involved with some men's work and some personal development stuff for a while when I read that book, but I really made a conscious effort to learn how to get in touch with my anger, to recognize that it was okay to get angry, that it didn't make me a bad person to get angry.

As I went through this process, and learned how to do that, amazingly, all my throat problems just all healed. As a matter of fact, I can't even remember the last time I actually had a throat issue. A lot of it is the result of my willingness to look at and address the fact that I had closed off that part of myself, and opening myself to just be real and authentic with the energy that's moving in me, especially that energy called anger, it freed me and helped me heal that part of myself. For those of you who are listening, I think this is really perfect and I want you to try to imagine which side of the coin you might be on, because I think it's a perfect example of how we as men are conditioned in our society.

A lot of us, as men, are taught to believe that anger is an acceptable emotion, and as a matter of fact, it's like, "Okay, he's just a man when he does that," it's all men raging out, and they act out as Terry mentioned. Again, the flip side is that there are a lot of us as men who don't know how to express anger in a healthy way. It can be debilitating so it's important that we understand that it's not about being right or wrong, good or bad, it's about being authentic with what's going on inside of you. Learning to be in touch with your emotions is an important part in transforming your life, so Terry, thanks for sharing that part of yourself. I want you to think about this now. As a result of doing the training, what did you learn about yourself that helped you start healing.

Terry:

Wow, I've learned so many things about myself and if I go back to the training, where I really kind of cracked open. What I realized about myself is that I did not trust other men. I did not trust other men because of the role model that I had in my father. The other big thing that I learned, Michael, was that the training kind of gave me a roadmap on why I do the things I do. It made me so much more aware that I was creating impacts and consequences by my behavior that was driven by me, it wasn't someone else. It wasn't like I had a Martian with a space gun to my head telling me to act a certain way. It was my choice.

I made these choices to act a certain way, whether to act out on my behavior or to repress on my emotions. Whether it was the messages I got from society, or whether it was something I learned from my father but the main thing was the choice: it's my choice. I took a lot from them and I'm still working on it, but probably the most significant thing I learned about myself is I have a choice and my actions, whether they're intended or not, have an impact on the people I'm have relationships with.

Michael:

That was one of the big lessons that I learned also as a result of doing the training. I had been involved in personal development work with men and women for a long time, and I always thought that I was a pretty open minded guy, and all of that. It wasn't until I did the warrior training that, like yourself, I realized that, to be completely honest I really didn't trust men. When I went to the training and I shined the light on this idea, I realized that for most of my life I didn't know what it meant to experience true intimacy with men. The reason I couldn't experience intimacy is because I didn't trust men and you can't be intimate without trust.

When I went through the training, it really helped me see how closed off I really was from men. It was easy for me to relate to men on the surface level but when it came to heart and guts, I was so afraid of men, and sharing with men and a lot of it had to do with that fear. As men, we don't want to be accused of being gay or we don't want to appear to be too weak or too soft or too wimpy, and all those are culture generated stereotypes about what it means to be a man. I had to be willing to examine all of those and this training really helped me do that. It really helped me look at all men and how I related to all men. It was really eye opening for me, because, as I mentioned, I had actually facilitated workshops and had written books on personal development but I'd never realized the impact of my cultural conditioning, my belief systems around men until I did this training.

That's why I believe this training is so, so important because it shines light on the foundation of a lot of male behavior in a way that I have

Chapter 5 ~ What Are The Benefits Of Men's Work?

yet to find through another organization that does men's work. I really honor them for this work because it was transformational for me to be able to now say, comfortably, to another man, I love you, and not just to say it with words but to feel it in my heart. That's the power of this training: when men allow themselves to get real and connect with other men, our lives change dramatically.

With that thought, Terry I'd like you to think about your relationships before and after the training. How did the training affect you and your relationships?

Terry:

I have to say that barriers dropped, walls crumbled, walls and barriers that were not allowing me to connect with individuals that were not allowing me to have an acceptance of what reality is. I thought in my mind that the world ought to operate a certain way, based on my belief system, because it was pretty much about me being in survival mode and being defensive, and thinking everyone was out to get me. The relationship that has changed the most is my understanding of intimacy. I like the word intimacy. I had no idea what that word meant; in fact, previously my relationship with intimacy only involved sexual contact. I had no idea it was about being in relationship and being intimate, "into me see", and actually having a relationship with someone where you can trust and share your deepest feelings.

What that does is allows me to be much more vulnerable and when I'm vulnerable, it allows me to open up and love and to trust. When I find out that other people are just like me, my life blossoms, it expands. I thought I was all alone with the way I thought and the way I acted. I realized, I kind of like the little saying that I use for men, specifically that we're all the same. It's like we're all a bunch of clowns on the same bus. We're all men.

Michael:

Nice. For me when I think about relationships before and after the training, as mentioned, I had done a lot of healing work meaning, emotional, psychological work before I did the warrior training. My relationships in general were actually pretty good. Again, the piece that was missing, I think you said perfectly was, as you said, the walls came down. For me as a result of the training, the walls really did come down, and it's like I allowed myself to open my heart for the first time in a way and at a level that I didn't know was possible. I allowed myself to be completely open. As a result of that, it removed a lot of fear, and it allowed me to experience true intimacy.

I think for men, generally speaking, we have been taught that our responsibility has always been to provide and protect, but no one taught us and told us that it's absolutely imperative that we learn how to connect. That's what this work allows to us to do, to learn how to connect and I believe that connection is what we truly, truly crave, whether we realize it or not. Until we remove the blocks that keep us from connecting, then we'll do things like have multiple sex partners, or get trapped up in materialism and all that, but there's always going to be something missing.

Someone once said that we all have a God-shaped hole in our soul, and the only thing that will fill it is God. Any time we try to put anything else in that hole, it simply makes that hole bigger.

Chapter 5 ~ What Are The Benefits Of Men's Work?

I believe that hole in our soul is that which connects us to other human beings. Until we learn how to actually open that hole a lot so that other people can see and touch us inside then we can never truly connect, but when we do, when we allow ourselves to connect and open our hearts in that way, then magic happens, because it's what I believe we all crave as human beings. We want to be loved, and we want to love and all these walls around our hearts make it impossible for us to do so.

Once again, I believe that this training is a doorway that we have to be willing to walk through. That's the work of transformation, to find the door, and be courageous enough to walk through that door without possibly knowing what's on the other side. It takes a deep level of trust to walk through this door sometimes but when we have other human beings that are there to support us, it really makes that job a lot easier to do.

With that said, thinking about the training before and after, what impact did the training have on your professional and work life? Did it affect those areas of the life also?

Terry:

Oh my gosh, yes. The big thing that comes up was as you mentioned before, that you were a people pleaser and that's a big thing for me. I'm a people pleaser, so my defense mechanism is to go along and tries to fit in instead of belonging. When I'm belonging, I'm accepting that people will accept me for who I am and when I try to fit in, I find myself coming up with behavior that's not very authentic. As far as my professional life what's really changed about that is I spend a lot less time on drama about trying to make sure that things get done as a salesperson. I was always concerned about making sure that I do things correctly and properly to get the sales, did I do enough. I found myself spending a lot of time double checking and not really accepting the fact, the sense of reality that this is enough, there's no need to do any more and I doubt myself. My self confidence level was at its lowest ebb before the training when I was always doubting myself. I'm always concerned about what people think about me. To sum it up, it gave me extreme amount of self-confidence and belief in myself, that who I am is enough. That sums it up, I think.

Michael:

I can really, truly resonate with that idea because for me, although I had been successful in a lot of areas of my life. As a result of doing the training, I also experienced this amazing level of confidence and I like to think that it allows me to have that walking on a cloud, I can do anything kind of feeling. It's hard to explain but there was this confidence that there is absolutely nothing I couldn't do if I truly set my mind to it. This time it wasn't about doing things to try to meet other people's approval but now it was about me doing it as an expression of who I am. It was about me getting in touch with my creativity and passion, and being able to share that with others.

Again, I had this feeling that I was walking on clouds and I've always been a really optimistic positive person. Some people even called me sort of Pollyannish because I consider myself to be an irrepressible optimist, but now I can actually say that I am an idealist, I am an optimistic person and now it's authentic. It's not that I'm doing it to try to impress or please other people, it's just an expression of what I am, as a man, as a human being.

I credit a lot of it to the training because it challenged me to really look deep within my own heart and soul. There's a wonderful saying I love that says, "If you don't go within you will always go without." This process is all about going within, it's about examining our deepest held beliefs, about who we are, about what it means to be a man, about what society has conditioned us to believe a man is supposed to be. When we blow up a lot of these belief systems and conditioning of society, in essence, we get to the core of who we are, and we are no longer bound and trapped by externals but are now driven from our core, from our soul, from ourselves, or what some people might call our higher self. That again was brought home as a result of doing the training.

I want you to think about this for a moment. As a result of doing the training, how did your relationships with women in general change? I'm not talking about intimate relationships. Did your perception of women change or did your beliefs about women change as a result of doing this training?

Terry:

They definitely have, not only with women but I think what has changed for me is just my whole view about people who are different from me. Whether it's gender or ethnicity or sexual orientation, or atheism or classism. I was in the road where it was all about me and I thought everyone ought to think like me, and act like me, and if they didn't, I really didn't understand that and there was obviously something wrong with them. But speaking about women specifically, the big thing that came up for me was the respect.

Being raised in my family, my mother was a role model in the positive and the negative ways that she raised me. That's all I had for a map on what women ought to be, though as it turned out she was a weak individual and pretty much let herself get pushed around and that's the way I was raised. That's the way I viewed women, that they were of a lesser sex and it wasn't until I did the training that I realized people are not all like me, and gained a better perspective on the multicultural age issue and about how we're all different but we're all equal. I gained a very different perspective on the fact that everyone that's different, including women.

Michael:

Awesome stuff. I know that for me as a result of doing the training I found that I could no longer tolerate men who in any way disrespected women. I Now, if I see a guy who is maybe downgrading women or treating women unfairly, I'm more likely to speak out and say something. For example, if I'm with a group of guys and I see guys catcalling women or something, I speak up and say that's not cool. Let's not perpetuate that type of behavior for men, and it really made me aware of my own sexism in a lot of ways. Here's a perfect example, immediately after I did the training, I went into an auto parts store to get a part for my car. It just so happened that there was a female at the counter, and there was a part of me that didn't believe she would know how to help me.

I kind of scanned around the store to find a guy to help me. When I did that, I became conscious of that and I recognized it was wrong,

Chapter 5 ~ What Are The Benefits Of Men's Work?

and I decided to wait for her and allow her to check me out and answer my questions. When I got to her to make my purchase, I actually apologized to her. I said, "I just want to apologize because my old conditioning had me thinking that you would not be smart enough to answer my questions about auto parts because you're a woman, and I'm sorry for that." I would never have done that before. As a matter of fact, I wouldn't have even had the awareness to recognize that it was a problem.

This really helped me see how unconscious we can be sometimes but again, the courage came from me being willing to acknowledge that and apologize to this woman. I've got to tell you, she smiled, and it felt really clean for me to be that honest with her and just to make, what I call make amends with her. I no longer hold that belief that women can't know about cars and auto parts. It takes a courageous man, an honest man to really get to that place where he can say these types of things but that's just part of our conditioning that says that women aren't competent in male-dominated fields like auto parts. That was a learning experience.

The next thing I want to talk about Terry is that, there have been some men who say that the training actually ended up being a spiritual experience for them. Can you relate your training in any way to a spiritual experience?

Terry:

Yes I can. Let me just say that my beliefs about spiritual aspects, my spirituality is my level of consciousness and before, I always pretty much shut down and thought about me and me only. My spirituality has blossomed where I'm now much more conscious, much more aware. I have a close relationship with nature. I believe there's not a lot of difference between nature and animals than and human men and women. I think the awareness is the consciousness of just what's around me and developing my spirituality was the big thing. I wanted to touch on something also, Michael, you said something before about your conditioning and it was a good reminder for me that there's no shame about the way I was, because I got those messages from society. I like that phrase, that I'm not responsible for me getting sick, but I must take responsibility for my own healing.

Michael:

Absolutely. For me, as a former atheist who really struggled with spirituality and religion for a very long time and then found a spiritual path that nurtured my soul, I came to understand that it was definitely a spiritual experience because my definition of spirituality is the moment-to-moment recognition and acknowledgement of my connection to something greater than myself. During the training, what I felt was this connection to everything, the men in the room, the different symbols, the signs, to the ground itself, the location. It was just this deep connection that I felt with everything.

It was like my whole body was just pulsating with this divine energy, whatever you call that energy, but it felt amazing. It felt amazing and so I made a point to connect to that feeling as much as I could. That feeling was again spiritual. I believe it is the core of who and what I am as a human being; it is my connection to The Source. When I learned to remove the walls that we were talking about earlier and opened my heart fully, then I created a connection to all there is. You mentioned that being in nature with animals helped you feel connected and I completely agree with you on that. Because in my reality, it's all connected. It's all the same and it's all part of the same thing.

It's energy and I believe that energy is spirit. When we really do the work and connect to that part of our self, I do believe that we are connected to the divine. You don't have to put any label on it, you don't have to go into any specific building to experience it, we just have to open our hearts to it and we have access to it. That's my experience.

Another thing that I really liked about the training is that it helps us open up to this idea that we have a mission. It invites us to recognize this mission and take that mission out into the world and, in our small way, impact the world. Did you wake up to a mission for your life as a result of the training?

Terry:

Before I did the training I had no idea. I talked about being so involved with myself and not thinking about other people. It's like mission of what we can maybe do for someone else. I got it, and my mission, my purpose in life is to create a world of love, trust and passion by teaching with my example. I use it as a barometer almost on a daily basis, especially when I feel like I didn't accomplish something, I'll think about my mission and how I live in my mission today, how was I loving, compassionate and trusting, and whether I model that or teach it. There was a big connection for me to come up with my mission and I have a lot of passion around that, and I've actually done some programs and some processes where I teach that.

Michael:

My mission was to create a world of love and understanding by loving myself and understanding others. That mission actually drove me to start this show, because I knew first and foremost that I had to learn to love myself. I had to get clean about who I am, get comfortable with who Michael Taylor really is, and, as a result of doing that work, I allow myself to try to understand others. I believe that understanding breeds compassion and when you get to understand others, it helps us heal the world. I really believe that. Having that mission statement is still one of the driving forces in my life to make sure that I'm staying on track to make a positive impact on the world.

With that, we start to wind down. Man, time flies when you're having fun. For those of you who are listening and thinking, what in the heck are these guys talking about, it's called the New Warrior Training Adventure by an organization called the Mankind Project. It's a powerful three-day weekend in which men come together to be supported, empowered and challenged to really discover who and what they are. There is a saying within the community that goes, "You can't get it until you get it," but you have to be willing to realize that there's something to get. If you've been piqued by this conversation and what we've shared so far, you have an opportunity to participate in this transformational process.

The new warrior training adventure is held around the world. I'd like to give you the web address so you can check it out. You can Google mkp.org is or The Mankind Project website and check it out. Don't just take our word for it. There's lots of testimonials on the website of men

Chapter 5 ~ What Are The Benefits Of Men's Work?

who have done this work. If you feel moved, if there's something in you that's what I call divine discontent where you just have this feeling that something is just not quite right in your life, then here's a great opportunity for you to do something that I know can and will change your life for the better.

Like I said, I'm a huge advocate of personal development programs and I actually consider myself to be somewhat of a workshop junkie. That's just what I do as a motivational speaker and author who has done countless training and I must admit that this training is unique. Again, I believe that this is something the world needs right now, because, as I mentioned, I believe that when we shift the male paradigm on the planet, the entire planet will shift for the better, and as an optimist I believe that that's happening. It's happening on a large scale that we may not see throughout our media. So if you're ready, I can assure you that the training is waiting for you.

Log on to the website at mpk.org and you'll find all of the details and directions for where to go, no matter where you are around the world. Just go to the website check it out, and if you feel moved, do something, take action, and transform your life.

Terry, I want to give you an opportunity to just speak from your heart. What would you say to the man who's been listening to this program and maybe feeling a little stuck in his life and maybe doesn't know what to do next?

Terry:

The first thing that comes up for me is to take a risk. Look at your life, and if it could be better, be willing to take a risk.

Michael:

Yeah, because I can assure you that with great risk comes great rewards, and if you're going to and willing to take a risk, I know that you will be rewarded in untold ways. It's amazing what can happen if you're willing to take that risk. It really boils down to trust, because there's no way that I can put into words exactly what the training is, but, as most men would tell you, if there is a part of you that simply trusts what we've been saying, listen to your own gut and let it guide you to the right decision even if you're not exactly sure what it is. If you just trust your own inner voice, that part of you that's saying, "You know what, I might be interested in this," if you hear that, if you feel that, then just trust yourself, and if it feels right for you, take a risk and do it.

Terry, I just want to say, thank you for showing up and sharing yourself and your wisdom. Now I just like to give you an opportunity to share any final golden words of wisdom.

Terry:

Thanks for the opportunity, Michael. This training has changed my life. If you don't believe me, call my partner, my wife and ask her. She can definitely vouch for my transformation as a result of doing this training. I have selfish reasons for inviting men because it transformed my life and I want to be around more like-minded individuals, who are more conscious, vulnerable, open, accountable men. That's what I want in my life and I want to encourage everyone to take a look at it and take the risk to see what you could do.

Chapter 5 ~ What Are The Benefits Of Men's Work?

Michael:

Perfect. That's a great way to sum it up; take the risk, transform your life. I just want to say, for all you men and women out there who are listening, is that this is one of those processes, one of those programs that I know can truly transform the world because it's transforming men's lives and when we do that, the world will change.

I am an irrepressible optimist with a passion for the impossible and I say anything is possible. If you're listening to this program, and your life is not completely where you'd like it to be, here's an opportunity for you to do something that will transform your life. Once again, thank you for tuning in to a new conversation with men. I wish everyone, joy, passion and excitement on this journey called life and know that life was meant to be good, but nobody said it was going to be easy. Terry, thank you so much for sharing this hour with us, and I look forward to meeting you very, very soon, my friend. Take good care of yourself.

Terry:

Likewise, thank you Michael, thank you for your listeners too. All right, good night.

Michael:

Good night, everyone. We'll talk to you next episode.

The benefits of men's work are immeasurable. You just have to make the commitment to yourself that you are willing to take that risk and transform your life. I hope you have received some fuel for contemplation from this interview. If it has piqued your interest and you would like to learn more, go to the Resources chapter of this book to take a risk and get involved.

You'll be glad you did.

Good luck!

We need to give each other the space to grow, to be ourselves, to exercise our diversity. We need to give each other space so that we may both give and receive such beautiful things as ideas, openness, dignity, joy, healing, and inclusion.

Max de Pree

Chapter 6
Diversity

A few years ago I participated in a 3-day seminar called the Sword & Scepter workshop (www.swordandscepter.com). The workshop is designed to support men in understanding their relationship to power and it helps men to access their authentic inner masculine power.

It is a powerful and transformative experience that I highly endorse with my highest recommendation.

After the workshop, one of the men came up to me and asked how it felt to be the only African American man in the workshop. Initially I joked with him and said I didn't even notice but I then decided to openly share my experience with him.

I explained to him that I had been actively involved with men's work for a very long time and had even written a few books on the subject of masculinity. As a result, I told him that I was completely comfortable in the situation and had no problem being open and vulnerable with the men in the group even though I was the only African American man in the room.

He then made a comment about how brave I was and how I had actually made a positive impact on him during the workshop as I had changed his perception about black men with my emotional honesty and authenticity. He finished our conversation by giving me a hug and thanking me for being at the workshop.

Our interaction confirms something that I've always believed to be true but that unfortunately gets overlooked because of our obsession with race. The truth as I see it is that all men are created equal. It doesn't matter what color you are or what religion you practice. It has nothing to do with your educational level or your socio-economic status. At our core, all men truly are the same. We all have thoughts and feelings. We have dreams and fears. We want to love and be loved and we want to know that our lives matter and hopefully we are able to make a positive difference in someone else's lives too. If I had to write a description of what a real man is this is what I'd say: "A man is a person of the male gender who knows who he is and lives a life of faith, accountability, integrity and responsibility."

Although I believe all men are created the same, I do not believe that all men are treated or perceived to be the same. This is the reason it is so important to have a conversation about diversity and the importance of it in our world.

As a man who happens to be black, I have been exposed to every type of racism, discrimination and victimization you can imagine. I have been physically attacked, had a gun pulled on me, had my life threatened, been called a wide variety of negative racial epitaphs simply because of the color of my skin. I know how difficult it can be to live in a society that has created a media-generated stereotype that black men are inferior so without question I am definitely qualified to share my opinion about diversity.

Chapter 6 ~ Diversity

My intention is to open a dialog about diversity by sharing my experience and hopefully by providing a new perspective on the challenges of being a man of color. My hope is by sharing, it opens the door to a dialog in which people can come together to figure out how to remove all of the hate and separation that is so rampant in our world today.

Steven Covey once said: "Seek first to understand and then to be understood." To fully understand the challenges facing men of color, I would like to share an excerpt from a video program that I put together titled, Shattering Black Male Stereotypes. The intention was to support black men in recognizing these stereotypes and empowering them to insure that they did not accept or act consistently with them.

By reviewing these stereotypes, I believe it can give you some insight into black male behavior and hopefully support you in "understanding" the importance of diversity and accepting people for who they really are.

Here are the 6 most negative media-generated stereotypes about black men. As you read the list ask yourself honestly if you've ever accepted any of these stereotypes as true.

1. Black men are an endangered species

Several years ago I was in a restaurant and overheard two apparently well-educated young black men having a discussion about the potential eradication of black men from society. In their conversation, they were discussing how they believed black men would be extinct in 20 years. When I approached their table and asked them why they believed this their response was: "Don't you watch the news? Black men are going to become extinct within twenty years. Either we are all going to be in jail or we're all going to be dead."

The reason they felt that way and felt so strongly that it was true was because of all the negative media images they are exposed to on a daily basis. The sad reality is that a lot of young black men feel this way and have already given up on accomplishing anything in their lives. Although I believe this is a small majority of black men, the fact that some of them even think this way is alarming to me.

This is why it is so important for the media to showcase the positive contributions and share the successes of black men. Without question, the media plays a significant role in how a person sees himself or herself and when a person is only exposed to negative images it will definitely influence their behavior. By showcasing more of the positive stories and successes, it can definitely help change the mindset of black males.

There are some who may argue that there is a lack of positive black male role models. To which I respond, there has never been a lack of black role models. There is only the lack of media exposure for those role models. There is no segment of society that does not have a black male presence. We have attorneys, doctors, lawyers, astrophysicists, and entrepreneurs, web developers, bankers, psychologists and the list goes on and on. So there isn't a lack of role models, there is simply a lack of exposure of them.

2. Black men are less intelligent

If you look at our country from a broad point of view, it wasn't that long ago that the "experts" claimed black people were intellectually inferior to whites. Even today there is still an implied message that this is true. For black males, this stereotype cuts like a double-edge sword. On one hand, young black men accept this stereotype and refuse to learn, and on the other hand, the truly gifted and talented black males reject their intelligence in order to reject the culture that they feel is holding them back. Speaking from my own experience, as a teenager I "dumbed down" and began skipping school because it was more important for me to have friends than it was to get good grades. Since the majority of my friends didn't excel at school I made sure that I fit in by not receiving good grades for fear of being rejected by my peers. Sad but true!

It's important to understand the impact this stereotype has on black males. But the solution for us as black males is to remove this stereotype by not only rejecting it and becoming educated but by also teaching our young black males that learning is fun and also very cool.

3. Black men are angry and violent

To confirm this stereotype, I'd like to ask you to remember the last time you saw a black male on television talking openly and honestly about joy and happiness. When was the last time you saw a black male on television sharing his true feelings of happiness, sadness or fear? As mentioned in the earlier chapter on men's emotional healing, men in general are conditioned not to feel; for black men, this sentiment is magnified. The media would have you believe that we are all angry and violent and hate our country but the truth is we feel and express emotions just like any other group of men. We are loving, caring, compassionate, sensitive and nurturing men who are also patriotic and love our country. Unfortunately, when the media constantly bombards the masses with negative imagery of black men, this stereotype is formed and too many people accept it as the way all black men are.

4. Black men can't be monogamous

If you pay attention to most rap music or watch their videos, it should be easy to see where this stereotype comes from. In too many cases, the music objectifies women and glorifies having multiple sex partners and the media definitely places a lot of attention on these images. Rather than point fingers and place blame, I will simply assert that black men are definitely capable of monogamous loving relationships and aren't afraid of commitment and intimacy.

5. Black men are deadbeat dads

As a father of three grown children who I absolutely love and adore, I'm sure I can speak for a lot of black men who are definitely remarkable fathers. There are so many negative statistics surrounding black men and fatherhood that I will simply say that we are no different than other races of men when it comes to loving and caring for our children. We miss our children, care for our children, inspire our children and have high expectations for our children that they will live rewarding and fulfilling lives.

6. Black men always use race as an excuse for failure

As this country continues to showcase the atrocities and unfairness that black men are exposed to on a daily basis, the reality is sinking in that race is still a major issue in this country. There are some people who believe we live in a post-racial America, which makes no sense to me because if it were truly post racial we wouldn't be having a conversation about race. The truth is, race does matter and we still have a ways to go in terms of race relations.

With that being said, I do not believe that race relations are actually getting worse in this country. Despite the apparent challenges we have in regards to race, I remain optimistic that race relations can and will improve in the immediate future.

There is a stereotype that says all black men use race as an excuse for failure and I want to dispel that stereotype right now. If you aren't a black male, it will be difficult, if not impossible, for you to empathize or understand the challenges of being a black man in America. This isn't using race as an excuse, it's an undeniable fact.

There is a scene in the movie *Crash* in which Terrance Howard plays a successful black man in Hollywood who is driving home one night when he and his wife are pulled over by a racist police officer. The police officer actually assaults him and his wife and there is nothing he can actually do about it. In the scene, he is absolutely powerless. If he resists, there is the possibility that he will get arrested or, even worse, get killed. By not being able to say anything or being able to defend himself, he begins to feel inadequate in protecting himself and his wife.

So what should he do? Should he attempt to save his wife from the assault of the police officer? Should he resist the officer's attack and risk becoming just another statistic of a black male senselessly killed by a racist cop? He decides to cooperate with the police officer and the police officer eventually lets him go. As he is driving home, there is silence between him and his wife. He obviously feels emasculated and humiliated as a man. You can feel the anger inside of him and there was no outlet for him to release it. When they arrive home, his wife actually attacks him for not protecting her and blames him for the entire incident. She accuses him of not being a real man and completely invalidates his experience and was unwilling to acknowledge the difficult choice he had to make in not resisting arrest.

This scene is the perfect metaphor for being a black man in America. I'm sure most black men can relate to the feeling of powerlessness that the character felt in that scene. Not only do we have to deal with outside forces like the police officer, we also have to deal with the inside forces of the people we care about who sometimes aren't supportive and understanding of the challenges we face.

So if you ever hear a black man saying that it's difficult for them to make it in society, before you judge him as playing the victim card take a moment and try and walk in his shoes. Although there will be some black men who cop out and use race as an excuse, the overwhelming majority of us won't and, despite the challenges before us, we will always find a way to succeed.

I'm not asking for your sympathy but I am asking for a little compassion for us because the challenges are real and we aren't just making up excuses or blaming society for some of our failures. It is becoming apparent that our justice system is unfair, our educational system is biased and our media continues to do an unfair irresponsible job in showcasing black men in general. But despite all of these challenges, black men continue to blaze new trails and in the words of Dr. Martin Luther King Jr. "We aren't where we want to be but thank God we're not where we used to be."

I hope you will take a moment and think about these stereotypes and see if you have accepted any of them as true. Ask yourself honestly and if you have, simply make a commitment to not judge a person based on what the media has conditioned you to believe.

At the beginning of this chapter, I mentioned that all men are created equal and I definitely stand by that statement. My experience has taught me that the beauty of doing men's work is that it challenges you to look at your deeply held subconscious and unconscious beliefs about men and then gives you an opportunity to change those beliefs.

Men's work also creates a safe space for men to openly discuss how they feel and what they think about men who may not look like them. It challenges men to look at their prejudices and assumptions about men who may not look like them. I have had some remarkable experiences dealing with race and diversity and one of the most memorable moments occurred approximately 20 years ago.

I was a facilitator at a program run by an organization called The Men's Counsel in Houston, Texas. During one of my breaks I was standing behind a curtain listening to another man giving a presentation on diversity. There were approximately 50 men in the room and they were all white. After the presentation, one of the participants stood up and began sharing some things he had learned from listening to the presentation. He shared how he had always been afraid of black people. He traced his fear back to his father who constantly told him that black people were inferior and they shouldn't be trusted. As he shared his story he began to cry. He realized that all the things his father had taught him were wrong and he felt an incredible sense of guilt for disliking black people. As he was sharing his story, he mentioned that he would like to ask forgiveness from a black person for his behavior.

He had no idea I was behind the curtain and he kept telling the presenter how sorry he was for his beliefs and actions towards black people.

All of a sudden, I walked out from behind the curtain and simply stood on the stage. The facilitator then asked the man if he truly wanted to heal his racial wounds and he said yes. He then asked me if I would be willing to participate in a healing exercise with the man and I agreed.

He invited the man on to the stage and I could feel his fear. He was really uncomfortable and didn't know what to expect. But I felt that he was sincere in wanting to move past his racism and judgments about black people so I remained open to participating in the exercise.

The facilitator then asked the man what he would like to say to me as a black man. Initially the man didn't say anything. He just stood there in fear not knowing what to expect from me. But the facilitator reminded him about what he had said earlier and he told him that he now had an opportunity to be honest with how he felt about black people and to make amends for his past behavior.

After several seconds he began to speak. He began by saying that he was sorry for listening to his father and believing that black people were bad. As I stood there with compassion and understanding without judgment, he started to recognize that he had no reason to be afraid of me. He continued by saying how sorry he was for using the 'n word' and for blaming black people for ruining America. He continued apologizing for a few seconds and then something happened. It was as if he opened his heart and allowed his true feelings out and all of a sudden he began crying uncontrollably. He began apologizing for some of the same things but this time he really meant it. This time he let his anger out, his guilt out, his sadness out and his frustrations out. He sincerely wanted me to hear and accept his apology and it was coming from his heart not his head.

I then approached him and hugged him. In his heart I believe he felt that I had forgiven him and in his own way he had let go of his anger and hatred towards black people. But most importantly I think he forgave himself and he was grateful to let go of all the hatred he had been holding on to for so long. By now he was really sobbing and all he could say over and over again was, "I'm sorry, I'm so, so sorry. Can you forgive me?" I continued to hold him and let him let go of his pain and I knew in his heart of hearts he had been transformed. Amazingly, a lot of the other men in the room were also crying and the exercise had actually helped a lot of the men heal.

America still has a ways to go in regards to race relations but I remain optimistic that a day will come when it is no longer a dividing issue. This experience with the racist man confirms that all people really can change but it takes a lot of courage to do so. The beauty of men's work is that it helps facilitate the healing process for men of all ethnicities and it is a powerful ally for this country to use to help in healing the anger and hatred some people feel towards people of other races.

"Darkness cannot drive out darkness: Only light can do that. Hate cannot drive out hate: Only love can do that."

Dr. Martin Luther King Jr.

In life we shall find many men that are great, and some that are good, but very few men that are both great and good.

Charles Caleb Colton

Chapter 7
What Men Are Saying About Men's Work

As an author of several books dealing with men's issues, I have been referred to as an "expert" on several occasions. It is a label that I'm not really comfortable with because to me it implies that someone knows all there is about a particular topic and I personally do not believe that this is possible. To me, an expert is simply someone who cares deeply about a topic and is willing to research said topic and figure out ways to improve that topic. This is what I do. I care deeply about the topic of masculinity and I'm willing to research and learn as much as I can about it and then I share what I learn in hopes of improving men's lives by providing them with insights derived from my research.

Over the past 10 years or so, I have had the privilege of interviewing several well-known "experts" on men's issues on my radio show and I have gained a vast array of knowledge and insights about men and the changing roles of manhood as a result of these interviews. Although I have had the privilege of interviewing experts and even having the honor of being considered one, what I have learned is that all men are experts in their own right and each man brings a unique perspective and insight about the challenges of being a man in today's ever changing world. They do not have to have a PhD or any certifications or diplomas.

They do not need special credentials or titles or tons of money in the bank. All they need is a willingness to get real. A willingness to share from their hearts not their heads and to be authentic in their sharing.

What truly inspires me is sitting with a circle of men and creating a safe space in which they can speak openly and honestly about how they feel, what they believe and what they think about being a man. When men get together and share their deepest feelings, their vulnerability, their hopes and dreams and their authentic selves, magic happens. Men's lives are transformed from the inside out and the world becomes a better place automatically.

With that being said, I would like to share some insights from some of the men who are a part of a virtual men's group that I have been involved in for several years. These men come from different parts of the world and vary by age, race, marital status, religion and social economic status. What we all have in common is a deep commitment to our own growth and healing and a willingness to share the lessons we've learned about ourselves to support other men on their journey. These men are my friends and associates and they are also my teachers and my students. We learn from each other and we challenge each other to grow. Our group meets approximately every two weeks through an online video community called the Virtual Men's Gathering and we meet for 90 minutes each meeting. I have grown to love and trust these men and I feel truly blessed to have them in my life.

Each of them brings a unique perspective on men's work and men's groups and I invite you to open your mind and your heart as you read their perspectives. I can assure you that their insights can be

Chapter 7 ~ What Men Are Saying About Men's Work

instrumental in your growth and provide you with insights that can support you in dealing with the challenges of being a man in our shifting masculine culture.

Michael Over

21
Single
Czech Republic

I used to hate males, especially those around my age, both in my early twenties and my teenage years. I hated them all. They only cared about sex, parties, alcohol, video games and acting stupid to get attention. I did what I could to push almost all of them away. I thought that all of them were the same and I was very judgmental. I refused to be like them. However, one year ago, I decided to give men a chance, that maybe, there were more men like me who had a deeper character and were interested in personal growth and spirituality. My ex-girlfriend introduced me to a man she thought I'd be good friends with. We had a chat and I decided to meet him. To my surprise after a period of time, he became the first man I called my brother. Then, in high school, I met a guy who was younger than me. We started to talk and discovered that we are on a similar path, even though our interests weren't exactly the same. About a year ago, I decided to give men a chance and tried to find something like an online group. I don't remember the details, but through synchronicity, I found the Men's Group community on Facebook where I contacted Michael Taylor. We did an interview and I was a bit nervous, impressed and honored. I was accepted into the Virtual Men's Gathering and I was really surprised. I have found older men who are on a similar path as I am. Men with whom I could share anything that was going on in my life, men that I could completely open up to and let my defenses down with. Men who have supported me when I need it the most. In a strange way, I started to see Michael Taylor as the father I've never had, but always wanted. When I saw two men fighting in our group, I couldn't believe what I was experiencing before my very eyes. I saw two men having a serious conversation dealing with an important issue in their relationship without cursing, without hating each other and without drama. I saw these two men being intimate and completely with their emotions and willing to work on the issue that troubled their hearts. Now, I am used to people walking away, numbing themselves, pulling the problem under the rug, but to see these two men facing their own reflections in the other made me realize how fortunate I am to be part of this amazing group of wise men.

One man in particular is in many ways like myself. We both struggle with depression, bad states, feeling down, trying to make it in our own fields, and seeing others succeeding and way ahead of us. As I described above, I used to be very judgmental about males before, I rarely go out with people and I am mostly by myself. But seeing another man going through the same stuff that I did and still do from time to time, I feel compassion towards my fellow man. I have never felt that before for another man and I am grateful for this experience. When I listen to my heart and perform a gesture that affirms that I care and that he is not alone and when I see him smile afterwards, it makes me happy.

For some, this may sound homosexual, but it isn't. Having a sexual attraction for another man and engaging in sexual behavior is, and so what? So what if a man likes men? If my heterosexuality is respected and I get no offers, then I am perfectly fine with speaking to gay men. At the end of the day, we are all human. Love and intimacy are our deepest needs, whether we admit it or we try to put up the image that we don't. It's like being the lone wolf, which I tried to do before and that path only leads to pain. I am really grateful that I found this group. I always find it incredible that I am respected and appreciated in our group despite the age gap. I am the youngest member and to be respected by older men brings me a lot of joy and gratitude. It makes me respect them that much more. Not everyone is ready to be a part of a men's group, not everyone is ready for men's work, which is basically just another part of self-discovery. But, it is a blessing to both the men who attend one and those they meet afterwards. I am not perfect, no one is. And yet, we are all enough as we are. It's easy to say, but to get to that place, that place where I see myself in this way, is part of the journey that I walk. There are many tests, many challenges and many obstacles, but at least I know that I am alive.

In many ways, I am still a child in my young adulthood. Inexperienced, emotionally wounded, struggling with childhood issues, still dealing with unmet needs from my childhood and the rage towards my father.

Before I became a member of our men's group, I was very arrogant. I created an image where I had it all figured out, I was unstoppable and all of that other stuff. Meanwhile I was only running away and hiding from my feelings, just like my "dad". I live in my head most of the time. I over think, I overanalyze and I use everything that I can to mentally hurt/punish myself, whatever I can find. I literally fish for this stuff. By being young and inexperienced, I feel alone, I feel like I am the only one who goes through this. But by sharing my feelings with my fellow men, I started to let my guard down. I started to open up and share how I truly feel and how I suffer under my mask of a top student in my class. I have everything that I need physically and could ever want. Great grades in school, a part time job that pays well and is fun for me, friends and a somewhat physically supportive family (they do what they can with what they have). And yet I am not happy… and yet I still suffer… and if I don't suffer, I make myself suffer. I feel like there has been a wall between me and my ex-girlfriend. As if I have erected a wall that I want nobody to go through; a wall that was tearing us apart. I am also very jealous because I don't feel good enough, because I haven't gotten my developmental needs met. However, I have taken responsibility for how I feel so that even if I want to control others and have them behave in a certain way, I don't do it, I take responsibility and I am doing the best that I can. But I frequently try to distract myself, even unconsciously at times, where I don't even know that I am doing it. Heck, I've been doing this in order to avoid writing my part of this book! By being open and honest in our group, I have received the gift that no money could buy, that no ass or tits could ever replace… trust. Many times, I put myself on the table, as I truly am and as I truly feel. I feel like I am putting my heart on a sacrificial altar, just waiting for the knife to pierce my heart. I sometimes feel like the whole world wants to collapse on me, even though I am in my room and there is silence all around me. I don't know why, but these are the emotions that I am experiencing on a daily basis. Holidays are the worst!

It is in our group that I began to trust men. And when I've put myself out there, and I shared myself, even at the risk of being hurt, laughed at and simply being exposed for who I am, I am no attacked but instead I am being appreciated, acknowledged and seen. I have been given a great gift: the presence of all of these great men every two weeks.

I believe that it is important to be a part of a men's group, or if you are a female then a female group, or even a support group. It is important to have a place where you can be yourself, knowing that you won't be judged, and knowing that you can just be you, the very essence of who You are. It has had a tremendous impact on my growth and it's better than anything I can do by myself.

My issues are primarily emotional and that's why they are so illogical.

Yesterday I thought about what it would be like if my dad would do this work… How he'd see his mistakes, feel shame about them and apologize to me… How much I'd love him and respect him… How I'd forgive him for all the things he did and did not do. I was trying to create an image in my head. An image that made me happier. Instead of accepting who he is pretending to be now… hiding behind his screens and papers, or working in his workshop, or around the house… But I know that I can't change him… I know that…. Fuck! I know that I can't make him into that image. The only one that I can change is me. That is my domain and that is my kingdom. I would be so happy if he'd do this work that has found me. But that is only in my head. As I was saying, those are only my own illusions, and they are sweeter than reality. I use my head because I have given up all other forms of mood alteration/addictions. But I have come to realize that the addiction is not the problem. It's just a symptom of something deeper, childhood issues essentially. I can't run away from myself, I tried. I tried so hard to do that, but there I was, always. Whenever I've lost my breath and whenever I've felt like I was being pulled through a meat grinder, there I was.

I distract myself very easily. This work is hard, going in and seeing all the things that have been there all along and I sometimes just lose myself and go chase some thoughts in my head, without even realizing it. But the only way out is through. As I'd leave my partner, the next one would mirror the same unresolved stuff to me. I have decided to see this through to the very end. Because, beyond all of this, beyond all of this shit, lies something that I cannot explain, it can only be experienced. A core, something that is pure even in the darkest and most vile people walking among us. Something that we all have in common. It is my desire that you touch your core someday, because when it touched me my life changed forever. I found hope in what has only seemed to be darkness before in a place where I did not think I could ever find it: inside myself.

Looking back on things, I see how I have changed a lot. I used to love destruction, violence, blood, gore and carnage in video games and Anime. But now I realize that this was just the expression of my own ruptured psyche. No wonder. Every day I felt like I was dying, like I wanted nothing more than the release of death itself. Living was and still continues to be painful at times. But I know that it's not life, it's not God, it's not other people, it's just my unresolved stuff. This brings the power back into my hands, but with power comes responsibility.

I have come to realize that money, fame, prestige, social status, all of these pale in comparison to real relationships based on mutual trust and intimacy, romantic or platonic. I also used to love war movies and I wanted to be a soldier myself because I wanted to kill and die, like the piece of meat that I believed I was. I used to shit on adults a lot before, but now I realize why things are the way they are: everyone is dealing with their own plates, even the most "perfect" looking ones among us.

I have compassion towards a man with similar issues. I feel you in your pain because I have been there and probably will be there again…in the shit hole that we both know.

Up to now, I thought that I was alone in my struggle until I saw a man go through something very similar to me, which made me feel like I am not alone, like I am not the only one going through all of this. It made me feel more connected and compassionate. This was the first time in my life that I have felt compassion towards a fellow man. I have even expressed my spontaneous urge to hug him. Although merely digitally, I saw his lips transform into a smile which made me really happy. It is through seeing him the way he truly was, vulnerable and struggling, that I was able to connect with him on that level.

Some of you may think that I am being too dramatic, or I am too emotional or melodramatic. Well, I am a human being. I feel, poorly, but I do. Being able to shoot a kid, or a woman, or anyone in the head without flinching or showing any emotion may look "cool" in the movies or video games, but in reality, this is merely just the mark of a destroyed individual. It is a mark of sickness and pain rather than something to strive towards. I was trying to do at some point. I saw emotions as a nuisance, as just another obstacle to destroy, get over or trample on, but that is not self-love. That is self-hatred. I have lived under its spell for far too long and I am sick of it.

I still feel like I am not good enough, even if all the evidence around me points to the contrary. Even if everybody assures me of the opposite, I won't deny my feelings. That is who I am right now. I may talk of a future self that may never come to be, yet another image I would like all of you to see. To cast my spell so that none of you expose the one who has been hurting all along.

I am not perfect. None of us are, no matter how much we try to reach that image that seems to distance itself the closer we get. Yet we are still enough, even in our imperfections and in all of our mistakes. And I cannot wait for the day when I'll feel this just as much as I understand it.

It sounds scary when you think about really being yourself, when you look at what you were hiding from all your life, when there is nothing for you to do and you are left alone with that feeling of emptiness and pain.

I'd like to share a moment from one of our calls when I was just beginning to access my emotions and the pain that I have been hiding from all of my life.

I allowed myself to be seen. Inner child dialogue: Child(c): "Are you forcing me to show myself?" Me: "No, I am begging you to give them a chance. I am begging you to give men one last chance." I put it all on the table, completely in my emotional brain, just barely able to reason and I reached out, I showed who I am and they all stayed. Everyone listened, everyone smiled, everyone paid attention. Michael Taylor: "I am your friend. I am not your dad, but your equal. We are all your friends." This was the most intense call of my life! And then we sang, played the guitar, laughed and had fun. In that moment of the crossroads, when I had a choice, to revert back, or to keep on going, to keep following my path, I chose my happiness. I chose my inner child. And in that moment, when I made that decision, my inner child told me, whispering very quietly: "You are my hero." It was an intense experience. I am going to speak only for myself, but I feel that it has been like this for all of us. Richard even said that we have all evolved through this. These decisions seem to come to all of us at some points in our lives. I have found out that trusting my intuition always works.

THE IMPORTANCE OF ADMITTING THAT YOU WERE WRONG

Being wrong is ok, and sometimes by admitting it you can save somebody's life and save many people from suffering horribly. It's just like an extreme example in the movies where someone is wrong and accuses the other party and the other party dies.

Attachments

I struggle with this one a lot. Holding on to moments of bliss and happiness, when someone has said something good or when someone has done something horrible, repeating these images and sensations in my mind over and over again. Keeping myself from the present moment. And yet life moves on, after every failure, after every heart break, after every loss, after every storm, life just keeps on going as if it was all a grand joke. Maybe it is and we are just playing a grand game with ourselves.

Meditation

I would define meditation as this: an activity that helps you get out of your head and focus on something else, which helps to remove mental tension which is kind of a norm in my life.

Meditation – finding the practice that works for you. For me, I am a born creator, it is the purpose of my life, it is who I am when I am stripped to my core, so morning pages are best for me. Morning pages are a form of stream of consciousness writing where you wake up in the morning and write 3 pages of whatever comes to mind. This is especially difficult for me because there is no wrong way to do them. They don't have to be organized, I don't have to be nice, I don't have to hold back, the goal is to write 3 pages and that's it, just like brushing your teeth, you just go on with your day afterwards. I learned about this from "The Artist's Way" by Julia Cameron. Lately I have been doing this in the afternoon or late evening because I just do not wake up so early anymore. Morning pages have the added benefit of clearing my mind as well. One night I was so full of energy that I just couldn't sleep, so I wrote about 8 pages on both sides, which is 16 pages. For others, it may be qi gong, yoga, sitting with tarot cards, talking about your feelings to trees, talking with animals, riding animals, taking care of animals, classical sitting meditation, journaling, or reflecting back on the day in the forest, automatic drawing, or simply expressing oneself through art. Whatever it is, beyond all the mediums that I could ever write down, I have found that it is important to identify what works for you is what works for you. You can choose to trust that, to trust yourself. Maybe for the first time.

Following the images of perfection

No matter what I did and no matter what I do, it has never been enough for my parents. I gave my best in school, while working out, or in competitions and when I learned about self-development, I did my best to become an image that my parents would finally appreciate, an image that would help me get their attention and love that my unconsciousness still craves for and mirrors in my relationships. I am starting to separate myself slowly, but the mere fact that I have to do this in order to remove these blocks to my happiness infuriates me. To have to do the work that my parents were meant to do. I don't know who'll read this, but I am writing this in the hopes that You, reader may have been in a similar situation, or maybe you are in this situation. It's hard, but You are not alone and You can do this. One of my primary struggles is self-sabotage, where I basically do whatever I can in order to keep myself from achieving what I want, or just simply resting. The cause of that is that I still believe that I am not good enough, and even though I mentally and logically understand this, I still continue to perpetuate these patterns. I realized that no matter what I try to do, I am unable to do this by myself. No amount of advice, or book information can save me from my own unconscious tendencies. Realizing this was the end of being a lone wolf and finally reaching out for help.

The importance of community

A teacher's book can give you the information necessary to achieve your goals if you apply it and you don't try in your own way. However, the teacher can help you go deeper than just his book. I have been living in isolation from people for most of my life, only meeting with a select few that I could trust and open up to. I compensated for this by watching YouTube videos while I proclaimed that I had no addiction. Back then, I didn't know how far the word "addiction" really went. I had a few episodes in my life where I reached out and even built a new social circle of great friends, but then I retreated into my bubble and isolated myself again. Still as I am now going out of my bubble once again, I can say from my own experience that relationships matter, relationships are important, both romantic and platonic ones. I found out that having a support system where I have people I can share my experiences, failures, mistakes, emotions, successes, goals and dreams with meets one of my deep needs that I have denied in the past. I was living in denial that I could do everything by myself and that I could conquer the world through my own "strength". I was upholding this persona that I had everything figured out while internally I was and still am really confused and crying out for attention.

Reaching out for help

As I have mentioned, I have tried to do it all by myself. But, looking back on it, it's really impossible to make it on my own, because even if I was stranded on an island, I am still dependent on the island and its sources of nutrients and clean water. The first instance that I can really remember when I reached out for help was when I tried to look for my first art tutorial online a few years ago. My social conditioning up until that point was "If I did not do it as a kid, I will never be able to do it." Yeah, but I was drawing anyway and I tried one video, looked at it, analyzed it, applied what I learned and I could not believe my eyes! I drew a great looking female figure! Or at least it was in my eyes and based on my skills at that time. This experience has opened up a whole new world where I could actually make my dreams a reality. I didn't need to reinvent the wheel, I just had to decide what I want, find someone who is doing it well and learn as much as I can from that individual. Now, I did hit my roadblocks that I am still dealing with, which manifest one way or another, unresolved childhood wounds, this can be found under many names in many books, but the simplest term really is socialization or conformity to the present dysfunctional systems that are in place. If you went to school, you know what I am talking about, if you've worked a typical 9-5 job, or you work in a "normal" work place, you probably know what I am talking about as well. There are exceptions to the rule of course, but just go outside right now and look at the first person on the street, look at their face, their posture and the way they carry themselves and then tell me, would all people carry themselves in this way if we lived in a healthy and functioning system? You know the answer. Back to the topic though.

Basically I realized through the experience with the tutorial that I could achieve my dreams with the help of others. As I was trying and trying to make things happen, I consistently sabotaged myself and I am very slowly overcoming that. I decided to reach out and seek help through therapy because I realized that I am basically just spinning my wheels and getting nowhere, or worse, going back to the same issues over and over again with very little progress. My will and courage isn't really useful in these particular instances, but now that I have a therapist with whom I can both share all of my issues, I get support and I leave with a manageable action plan that I can implement right now, I am finally getting somewhere. The bottom line for me is that I can be independent in some ways, but knowing my limits and asking for/reaching out for help has given me hope where there was previously only a wish for everything to end. When we are separated and fighting, we are weak, but when we can stand together, we can do that which we set our minds to together.

Emotions

For me, my emotions were my enemy, something to fight, something to destroy, something to not listen to, a menace, a hindrance, an obstacle, a weakness and an annoyance. It is only recently that I am discovering that my emotions have value, that I can trust them and that every emotion is a response, therefore it has a cause. My sadness, my healthy shame, my guilt, my anger, my joy and happiness, they all make me who I am. Human. The last two are especially challenging for me because I didn't even know that happiness and joy existed until I attended my first high school. Where I live, we have specialized high schools.

The importance of emotions

My father rarely expressed emotions in my life, other than passive aggressive anger and manipulation. I saw him cry when someone from our family died. Otherwise he just lives behind a screen, newspapers, or the work around his house. Therefore, I was never really able to bond with my father other than the few times when we played video games together, which was a very long time ago. Once he stopped playing them with me, our relationship, what little we had, was over and it has gotten progressively worse. I can barely communicate with him, he is a perfectionist and demands perfection from me in everything that I do and I was never able to measure up to his expectations. Because he rarely expresses his emotions, I am unable to connect, or relate to him. My family lives together, but separately, each member in their own room, each behind his screen and each closed in his own world. When I see somebody cry, sad, shamed, angry, pissed off, furious, numb, depressed, or happy, I can both relate and know how to interact with the individual. They also help me empathize with the person if I have gone through a similar experience and even if I have not because I know how it feels.

Emotional connection

Both of my grandfathers are dead. I wasn't at the first one's funeral, but I was at the second one's funeral. I did not cry in either case, though these were also the only two times that I saw my dad crying and expressing how he felt. When I was at the second grandfather's funeral, there was nothing again. I didn't lose anything because I had no connection to him to begin with. However, I was kind of horrified at the funeral because of what I have experienced. There were a bunch of people there and a few family members. Everyone was crying. I was in the front row with my family and to my right was the wife of my deceased grandfather's son. I looked at her and told myself, "I'll support her" so I hugged her, She then looked at me and said, "Who needs the support now?" I was shocked for a moment and did not answer because it was not me and I couldn't just say that out loud. The main reason for this was because I had no connection with my grandfather to begin with.

The devaluing of emotions

I hate it when people say, "Oh, you are just too young, you don't know anything, you shouldn't be depressed, there are people in Africa…" and on and on and on, devaluing how I feel in the present moment. I mean seriously, when I am depressed and somebody tells me that I have nothing to be depressed about, I get angry and my impulse wants me to attack that person or walk away because I am being devalued, my emotions are being devalued and because I can't trust the person who said these words, I get defensive. Teens are usually like that as well. The more loving thing to do is to listen and reflect and validate these emotions without giving advice that wasn't asked for, in my experience. Or, when somebody is pissed and they tell me, "I am not in the mood," well then I let them be and sure enough, the next day or week, they are alright and life goes on. Emotional intelligence is something that I am just getting into and learning about, but now I know how important it is to communicate and live with other people on this planet.

Choices/decisions – following your own path when everything and almost everybody wants to be against you

When I was about 11 years old, a new friend introduced me to the world of fitness. A new gym has opened in our town and we went there to work out. He stopped going while I remained and worked out. I had no idea what I was doing, so I went to every machine that was there and did what I could. I usually stayed there for over 3 hours. I was the one who made the decision to go there consistently. Nobody forced me to go there, although people commented on my technique and what I was doing without me asking for it, which was rather annoying. It was my decision to do it consistently.

When I discovered the internet and a way to improve my artworks, as I have mentioned above, it was my decision to try it, it was my decision to listen to myself and see where it could take me. It was my decision to protect everyone from the monster that I believed that I was, trying to be a hero by sacrificing myself like a main character in a fantasy movie. And it was my decision to rise up from my own grave that I made for myself and get out of my shell to try to live again, to give life another chance.

The courage to keep on going

When everything goes to shit and there is no hope in sight, it is up to me, to move through whatever is happening, no matter how much I feel it consumes me. Of course, I am eternally grateful for all the support of those who cared and did their best for me. Courage and a strong will is like a muscle; it is hard at first, and I personally felt like there was just a barrier that did not let me go through, but I went for it anyway and I became stronger because of that. It's just like when I went to the gym. When I was at home and I was about to go, my mind was saying, "Oh my god, I don't want to go there, I don't feel like working out, I am tired, I can't do this." And you can add your own two cents there. However, when I moved my feet and showed up in the gym, I did not want to go home afterwards.

The hero in my heart

When I was standing at the edge of a cliff, ready to end it, being sick of life, I felt my heart and I heard a voice that gave me all the reasons to stay. My comic book series, my artwork, my goals, my dreams, my friends and all the things that are waiting for me in the future. When I feel so much pressure in my life that I feel like I am going to break, I can always sense something inside of me that just says "Keep on going, it will get better, I promise." Because of that voice and the numerous experiences that I have had, I came to the conclusion that I can't kill myself, that that is just not an option for me, so no matter how hard it gets, or how dark my life may be, I'll always keep on going. That is what I have chosen.

My failures and how I lost everything twice

As I reflect on the short bit of life that I have experienced, I can see that every failure has been a learning experience. For example, when I tried to start two businesses and failed with both of them, I learned that starting a business from scratch takes a lot of time, years in fact. It takes a lot of effort, dedication and motivation to make it happen. Neither one of them were compelling to me and I was in it for the money because I didn't want to go back to my parent's house as a failure, which I was forced to do because I didn't make it. I had to learn my lesson the hard way, but that is what it took. This experience has given me enough clarity to know who I am and what business I really want to build. It is a dream now, but every day I am getting closer to it in my own way. Even though I may be doing something unrelated to it, I am still working towards my dream and the vision for my life.

Risks

Every action, even going to the toilet in the morning, carries its own risks, which translates into worrying and getting into my head. When I decided to go to art school, the 3rd school that I'd attend, I took the risk of not being able to find a decent job even with the degree that I'd attain; it was literally up to me. Almost everyone was against my decision, my teachers and my parents, but I knew what I wanted to do for a living. I knew my purpose, I knew what gave me joy, what made me really happy and so I followed my heart's calling and I crashed into my own internal beliefs (this is explained in the next paragraph). I am still willing to do what it takes. In fact, this is the primary reason why I still keep on going. This is my purpose and one day, I wish to co-create a life where I can play, have fun, explore the world and make a living doing that, just like so many others are already doing. It's not that rosy I know, but I can do it.

Sacrifices

The hardest decisions that I have made in my life have been those where I had to sacrifice something that I really cared about. When I decided to go to art school, I had to give up my awesome social life. It was the first time when I was so happy socially and giving that up wasn't easy, but it was a small price to pay for the joy of moving in the direction of my purpose. Once I was faced with going to art school and fearing what I may do in my current state, as I believed myself to be a monster, the risk of protecting those I really cared about from who I thought I was, was the experience of severe shame of being a dropout, most likely not finding a decent job and God knows what else. However, the risk was even greater because I had discovered my joy and I was following my purpose. I felt alive, I felt like I was really alive for the first time in my life, I was enjoying it, but this choice was certain emotional death. So in a way, I have sacrificed myself and I wanted nothing more than for death to take me. I tried what I could, but I could never bring myself to end it—even with nothing but a disappointed family and an existence of emotional and psychological anguish, my heart was still beating. After about two years, I decided to try again, to give my life another shot, my Plan B was that I could just find a mediocre job to just get by, play online video games and live behind the screen for the rest of my life and wait for my inevitable death. And now I barely touch video games because they just bore me to death!

Surviving emotional death and the willingness to try again

No way out—Suicide is not an option anymore.

Now I am going to be brutally honest here. I survived this emotional death by disassociating from my situation and living through what I saw on my smart phone screen; it gave me relief, the only medicine that I could quickly reach out to. Obviously this wasn't the best thing to do, but that was how I went about my depressing days. I still marvel at the fact that I was still doing calisthenics at that time.

My life has gotten a lot better and I have grown in the process as well. I still have my dark days, or weeks, I still experience struggle and pain. I am still human and my heart is still beating.

Boysen Hodgson

45
Married
USA

Lessons from Men's Group

By Boysen Hodgson

Are you willing to sit in the discomfort of truly being seen, and truly seeing yourself?

Can you imagine having a group of men to help you open your soul, develop your innate potential, and have an impact on the world around you?

These are challenge questions for joining a high-functioning men's group. A men's group can be a place secure enough to help you see through your own bullshit and glimpse, through squinted eyes, the brilliance of who you are.

To understand the impact that being in a men's group has in my life, I have to go back 30 years.

My parents loved me. I had brothers (eventually five of them) surrounding me. I lived in a safe, if isolated, part of upstate New York. For some period of my life, I had a 'normal' childhood. I have fond memories of play, of being out in nature, of friendships. I had a center, a strong sense of place from those days on a small stretch of gravel road in the country.

My parents divorced when I was ten. In this, I am not unique. It was 1981. Both my Mom and my Dad embarked on a decades' long search for themselves, through multiple new marriages and divorces, new children, houses, schools, churches, and towns, sports cars and horse farms. I had step-parents and step-siblings. The stability I thought would always be there quite suddenly vanished. It was replaced by a world characterized and plagued by sporadic chaos and constant complexity.

Love seemed to me to be a very fragile and capricious thing. I learned to cope. What felt safe was to be recognized for being nice, 'good,' smart and cooperative. I hid all else. I buried the rage at my parents, my situation, bullies, Wednesday nights and every other weekend. I hid from the grief and sadness and confusion that I felt every day. I escaped using whatever meager tools I had. There's a lot I don't remember.

And there are many things I remember that still bring shame and grief, especially as I grew into puberty.

Again. I am not unique.

When I was a teenager, I started reading about self-help. My Mom had an affinity for esoteric writing; it was part of her own search for meaning. The shelf where I started my inner journey had names like Herman Hesse, M. Scott Peck, Robert Pirsig, Alan Watts, Edgar Cayce, Thich Nhat Hanh, Richard Bach, Shirley Maclaine, Dan Millman, and many more I don't remember. I read a lot. I skimmed a lot.

I absorbed. To this day, three decades later, the language of those volumes still comes back. It's the baseline, and I'm deeply grateful for it.

But there were problems with this.

In the mid 1980's, I was a pop psychology dilettante. I skimmed the surface of deep pools picking up just enough to protect and cover the abyss of my vulnerability. Those books helped assuage the terror of those feelings I wasn't prepared for or taught to experience as a boy.

I was very good at hiding out. My love of books became another place to hide.

I didn't have this language back then, but I was grooming myself to be a dutiful practitioner of the spiritual bypass. I used platitudes to avoid depth of feeling. I used my 'wisdom' to belittle others and avoid intimacy in relationships. I used my 'non-attachment' to avoid responsibility and accountability.

Maybe you can identify. There is a way to absorb a whole bunch of information and still lack wisdom. The wisdom only comes in the lived experience … in the application of knowledge … in practice.

Among the books there on the shelf was a thin volume called "Das Energi" by Paul Williams. I have owned half a dozen copies of this book through the years, giving them away, losing them, buying another.

One page simply says,

"You know what has to be done. Why don't you do it?"

These days, this kind of truism is the stuff of popular advertising. Embrace the swoosh, right? At 17, as the boy I was in 1987, it was revolutionary.

I have, by my own choices both conscious and unconscious, spent years running away from what I have known has to be done. Why? Because at some level I believed that I would be abandoned, shunned, and attacked for being who I am. And because I had internalized a message that unless I rigorously and vigilantly 'held it together,' it would all fall apart; the chaos would destroy me.

And much of the chaos had to do with the story I inherited about what it meant to be a man.

I achieved. I did well in school. I was widely regarded as a kind and compassionate person. People complimented my parents on how nice of a boy I was. As I grew older, I never had trouble getting girls to connect with me, 'fall' for me, or have sex with me. And I think for many of them, sex with me was an empty experience. I think women felt the truth even if they couldn't name it, that they were hungrier after the intimacy than before it. They would try to get more, to bring me out, but that level of connection was one I didn't know how to create.

I never had trouble getting employers to hire me, and I always aimed low. I got jobs where I could keep my sense of superiority without taking significant responsibility. It was a low-risk existence. I built a life. And deep down I think I feared I would be consumed by the emotions I had repressed. And I thought I was different than other men.

Beyond my identity as a 'good guy,' I was terrified of my potential for harm as a man. I didn't trust men. I had been shown in my life over and over that men were not trustworthy. That given the opportunity, they would hurt others to serve their personal desires.

What emotional truth I felt, I externalized into my relationships with women, placing a burden on those women who chose to get close me. 'Where are you?' was a question I heard over and over. I was kind, but distant. And when a woman got too close or too real (like … human), I was gone. Often I left a fog of pseudo-psychological new-age bullshit in my wake.

Over and over, I avoided taking risks. I kept waiting. Maybe the next random page of the I-Ching would give me what I needed. The next new philosophy would reveal the way. The next hardly touched spiritual hobby would break the old pattern. The next workshop would make me feel good enough to step outside of my terror of being seen (and therefore exposed). Sometimes I would wake up through a peak experience and the high would stay with me for a period of time. Pretty soon though, the inertia of unauthenticity would kick back in.

So what does this have to do with a men's group? Stay with me.

The first time I attended a men's group, I was about 27 years old. I went because my relationship at that time was in rough shape. I was desperate to show her that I would 'do something' to fix it. I showed up on a Monday night with no idea what I was getting myself into—and no idea what I might experience.

I was, by and large, unimpressed. I made up stories about why this was true. I constructed an elaborate justification for why the men in the group weren't men who could help me, how I couldn't trust them, how they wouldn't understand, how what I wanted felt deeper than what I saw, how I had already evolved beyond them. This was a symptom of my bypass.

It's clear to me now that I simply wasn't ready to do what needed to be done … to risk exposing my soul and telling the truth. The men in that group never had the chance to know me because at that point there was no way I would risk being seen. I was unready to know myself. And true to form, I would not stick around long enough to risk it.

I dismissed it. I went back to sleep. My universe got smaller. I continued to use the books that I started reading as a teen to shore up a growing avoidance of the truth: about my relationships, my wants and needs, my vision for the future. What I was unready to admit, the truth that would eventually set me free was that I actually needed men to help me break through the armor I had created and was continuing to polish each day.

Years passed.

My next connection to a men's group came through the ManKind Project's New Warrior Training Adventure.

Starting in 1996, while I was hiding out and my world was growing smaller, a number of men in my family completed a weekend program called New Warrior Training Adventure. My brother Jay, who is 18 months younger than me, was the first to do it. Each man who went through it invited me. And each time I was invited I ran. They didn't tell me what happened, but how they showed up after doing it was terrifying to me. They were honest about who they were. They were much more willing to confront me and each other.

Deep down I longed for the challenge, but in the real world I could not face the truth of what I was continuing to choose. It would be almost 8 years before I would be finally ready to submit to the voice inside me that grew louder and louder over time.

I paid a price for those years lost. Because I was afraid to risk, I didn't push myself to create the kind of work I wanted. I held jobs that didn't support me, and that provided no future growth. I stayed in a relationship that was unhealthy, co-dependent, and often emotionally abusive. I had consistent recurring issues with pornography that I hid and lied about. I was largely disconnected from my family because I was deeply ashamed and because when I was in contact with my family, my relationship was more difficult.

Even in those years, I held onto the aspirational vision of a different world for myself. There were aspects of my life that, even now, I remember with warmth and longing. I have seen this to be true in all the men's work I've done. Nothing is ever all bad. The seed of brilliance is there, the conscious life wants to be manifest, but the inertia of the inauthentic life is powerful.

And the pain got worse.

In 2002, my Mom died after a long battle with cancer. When she died I was not there. She died before I got honest. I think she died knowing that I was lost and struggling. This new shame drove me. It woke something deep within me and it would not be long before I found the strength to finally begin acknowledging the truth. This lead me to individual therapy and helped me to finally end the relationship I had been in for much of my 20s. My whole life started changing. Truthfully, it often sucked. It hurt. It was hard every day to see how I had damaged myself and hurt people around me.

Slowly, I began breathing again.

It would not be long after that when, after a chiropractic appointment, the doctor took me out in the hall, commented on the changes he was noticing in my life, and asked if I had ever heard of the New Warrior Training Adventure. I laughed. I believe I told him to fuck off. And then I told him I would sign up.

Six months later I would complete the New Warrior Training Adventure.

If you haven't experienced this initiation, put this book down, go find the closest one to you, and sign up for it right now.

By that time, I was already in a new relationship with the woman who is now my wife of 10 years, Kendra. There was something inside me that recognized that unless I did the work to heal my relationship with men and manhood, I was doomed to repeat the litany of horrors that I had witnessed in my family.

The experience of those 48 hours cracked the armor I had spent 20 years building. My friend and brother Mark Morey calls it 'the stone shirt.' What I witnessed in myself and the other men on that adventure altered my view of the world. It is now impossible for me to believe that I am alone in my experience, or that other men will not be able to understand what I have been through.

Over the last 12 years, that crack has been stretched, opened and widened. I have crawled out of my mental and emotional prison. It allowed me to create an authentic relationship with myself first, then with all those I love, and in a way, with thousands of people I will never meet.

Without a men's group, I believe I simply would have found a new patch to cover the hole and kept moving on with the distant life I had built for myself. This evolution, from closed to open, from desperately hidden to fiercely awake, has happened through men's groups.

It is the seed of all that I have now. An amazing and talented wife, a gracious home, two incredible and powerful children, men that I rely on and turn to, and always more possibility.

Here are just three lessons I've learned (trust me there are many, many more):

My shame is not my own

Many men walk through the world believing they are somehow miraculously unique in their feelings—especially in their shame. Shame is a cancer in male culture. It is the powder in the keg of men's violence. It is the root of the double life lived by so many men. When I see the latest politician arrested on drug charges after passing harsh anti-drug laws, or exposed as a sexual predator after spending decades preaching 'family values' , or being outed as gay after railing against homosexuality, this is the crop that we reap from men's shame long buried.

Shame is the felt experience that says 'You are bad'. It is the belief that you are somehow broken or universally guilty. It is the thought that says, "You can never let them see this weakness." It is the voice that tells you that you are is not good enough, not worthy, not valuable for who you are. I lived in that shame for decades. I have come to see in the eyes of hundreds of men that this shame is something we share.

It is embedded in the collective unconscious mind of men. It is persistent. It drives many of the most destructive and violent actions inflicted on the planet. Without the need to prove that I am worthy, that I am not broken or fundamentally 'bad', I believe that peace is possible on our planet. I have learned this from being in men's groups.

I have been with men to witness their shame and seen them let it go. I have heard men share the deepest recesses of their hearts, the parts of themselves they believed were irredeemable. And I have seen these men collapse into the depth of their grief with the simplest of words: "Are you ready to let this go?"

It is possible. You could have this too.

I can only grow to the extent I risk

You will have to risk looking foolish if you ever hope to grow. I still struggle to allow myself the freedom to look less than put together. I learned that if I looked good, it would be easier to hide what was really happening. It is only through risk that anything will change. There are many ways to learn this lesson and I have experimented over the years with risking in multiple arenas in my life as a man. I'll break this down a little more to illustrate.

Many men are comfortable taking risks in some areas, but frozen in others. Integral philosophy talks about "lines of development." There are many, but the ones I'll mention now are Physical, Intellectual, Emotional, and Spiritual. The masculine is encoded in our culture to be fairly comfortable taking physical risks and (depending on context) intellectual risks.

We encourage men's risky physical behavior. We actually expect it. It is one of the prices of entry to 'alpha' manhood. These risks can lead to some outstanding human achievements. I fully own my love of physically pushing myself, sometimes in some pretty foolish ways. I have had to learn to temper my physical risk taking so that I would not be injured. There is a flip side to the physical risk as well: the physical risks that men take with their bodies with food, with lack of care and attention, with abuse of so many different types of substance. Many men abuse their physical bodies through neglect and addictions to food, drugs, alcohol, sex.

Stuff the pain. Suck it up. Don't be a pussy. This is part of how the masculine enforces the hegemony that drives men to truly dangerous and unhealthy behaviors. From the extremes of head trauma in professional sports to the epidemics of obesity and addiction, to the ongoing horror of domestic violence; physical violence and risk-taking kills men, women and children.

To a lesser extent, we also encourage intellectual risk taking in men. In some contexts, this is fundamental to our evolution as a species. Exploring the edges of the mind and pushing the limits of what we, as miraculous creators, are capable of manifesting in the world is sometimes equated with prowess. Certainly in the tech world and many business pursuits this is true. This is frequently less celebrated in the mainstream these days. The dumbing down of American society and the avoidance of intellectual risk is rapidly leading the human species to the threat of extinction.

However, the elevation of the intellectual over all other lines of development has also lead humanity (and men) down the path of no longer being able to identify deeply with the emotions that are the primary underlying motivations for our actions. The myth of the rational actor, in the economic and social realms, has certainly damaged our society. The elevation of the intellect has also created generations of men (and women and children) who are disconnected from the natural world, trapped "in their heads". This isolation has created a desolate sense of disconnect among the human species.

Spiritual risk-taking is harder to define, but let me put it this way: taking a spiritual risk might look like opening yourself to the possibility that all things are connected, and that our unity as a species as beings on a finite planet demands that we make room for other species, other kinds of people, and other ways of experiencing the world.

The risk that men are most afraid to take is emotional. It is the risk to their hearts. It is a risk to the stories they are told are the essence of masculinity. It is a risk to the internal stories they have lived with since they were boys. What 12 years in men's groups has shown me, and what I have experienced, runs contrary to the cultural story we are told by society. Men's hearts are very close to the surface. Tragically, they are covered in a layer of dense and brittle armor. Dense because for many of us, it is very difficult to penetrate. Brittle because with all the show of invulnerability, men are frequently and often easily shattered.

This, I believe, is our greatest hope.

One of our deepest fears is that the shattering will destroy us. That without the layer of armor, without the masks we have made for ourselves, we will be consumed by the ravenous longings that our repressed emotions have concealed.

I believe that if I become angry, I will rage and hurt those I love. I believe that if I grieve, I will lose myself in the grief. That if I feel the powerlessness and fragility inherent in the human condition, I will lose the will to act. That if I allow the tenderness of love, compassion, forgiveness and joy to emerge, I will lose the hard edges I have spent my life honing in order to believe I was safe. These stories are, in all I have seen, never true.

My safety, my growth, my evolution depends on vulnerability. Without risking this vulnerability, there is no way to grow.

Every circle has the potential to blow my heart open

Men's group has brought me into relationships with men who I would never have met in any other way. Men come from wildly different backgrounds, from different countries, from multiple generations and multiple traditions, and yet we connect.

Every new configuration offers something unique. There are conflicts that arise, interpersonal flames that pop up. There may be language barriers, technology barriers, time zone issues. There are clashes in life philosophy, in stimulus processing strategies, even in basic beliefs about masculinity and manhood. And yet the group moves on. This is the power inherent in the circle. That with all that could pull us apart, we return over and over to what brings us together. We come back together to fiercely love one another and to fiercely love ourselves.

In each conflict is the seed of revelation. In each man's truth there is the possibility that I will glimpse yet another layer in my own emergence.

I am reminded of many incidents over many years, each unique and each universal. A man will be speaking about something in his life, stringing words together in the narrative by which he defines his limits and something will shift in the group. A disquiet enters the space between the words. And when the group is in its finest rhythm, meeting the true purpose for which it was conceived, someone will speak to the change. He will speak to what he sees, or ask a question that invites the speaker into a clearer view of himself.

"I'm noticing something, can I ask you a question? I'm seeing something in your eyes as you're talking about this ... tell me more about that."

And if a man is ready to let the circle be a light shining on him, his shadow will be cast there in the quiet of the space and he will turn to face it. What he has been hiding from in himself will be there in the room. And he will speak to it.

What I have said in those moments has changed my life forever.

Each circle has the power to blow my heart open. Sometimes I am the man speaking, sometimes the man asking the simple question, and sometimes I am the man sitting silently, bearing witness.

On another page in that thin volume by Williams, it says:

"(((DO IT)))"

Richard Arsic

52
Single
Canada

Hello all! First, I want to thank Michael Taylor for being the catalyst of this creation. My hope is that the words shared in this book by my dear Virtual Men's Gathering will shed some light on your path to freedom. I know it can be daunting and filled with challenges. Only the most courageous of men are willing to embark on such a journey. Since you are reading these words, I would consider you to be one of those men. Or perhaps you are a woman looking to gain deeper insight into men's work. Please share what you glean from this text with others, especially men. The world needs more strong, reliable, compassionate and loving men. Thank you for your service and enjoy!

The importance of men's work in this day in age, I believe, is paramount to our sustainability as a thriving human race. Many articles and books have been written about how men are the cause of much of the world's issues. I would have to agree. We will also be the cause of the final catalyst for change as we awaken.

We, as men, hold much of the power in this world and carry the physical force to enact our will. Unfortunately, that will is oftentimes wielded from a wounded inner psyche or inner child. A child that was taught at an early age to "stop crying", "be a man", "men don't cry" and "don't be a sissy or a girl", the depths that this last statement burrows into goes deep into our beliefs around women. What is that statement actually saying about our women—that showing feelings is attributed to women and that is somehow bad? Every time I hear a father, or mother for that matter, say "don't be a sissy", it drives me nuts. I suppose that is still an unhealed wound that I must also tend to.

It is of my opinion that women are the most resilient creatures on the planet! They bleed every month to make room for the new possibility of life. They hold life in their scared chalice and birth it into the world. Every person on the planet came to be through a woman. And somehow we have come to think that women are weak, less than, unequal, sexual objects and many more derogatory adjectives that we use as men to invalidate each other.

Let's look at greed, corruption and competition that is playing out in all facets of our lives. I believe this to be a symptom of the wound that we all carry as human beings, not being good enough or worthy. Religion, governments, media and many other things that show up in our day to day lives use this tool to control us. Whether it is the new car because your neighbor has one or going to church on Sunday to be redeemed, it all adds up to the same thing! That somehow I am flawed and these "things" will miraculously repair my imperfections. This runs rampant in our society and is a foundation of how we operate as a whole.

I see competition as having a large stake in how we show up as men in the world. Whether it is the friendly jab in the change room, proving yourself at work or how we demean each other sitting around the card table, competition shows its ugly head everywhere. If my words are stronger than yours in any given exchange, I win. If I am able to overpower you with my intellect, physical strength, money and/or the toys I have, I win. Wall Street is a prime example. Look at politics for another. Look at the childish games that go on in your church assemblies. This runs rampant throughout society and inner circles.

As men and women start to awaken to how these things play out in our lives, we will see that society does not reward the loving, nurturing ones, but the competitive, greedy and corrupt ones. From this new perspective, we can start to model the change that we desire to see in the world. As our actions ripple out, it will affect all we touch, sometimes in a good receptive way. Or sometimes it may challenge your world view and offer a new perspective, perhaps a new lens to view life through. This can be daunting and not for the faint of heart. Perhaps this resistance is what keeps many men stuck in their world of safety.

Over the years I have witnessed women attending spiritual awakening and new age events in droves. In my opinion, women are showing the way. They are leading the way into the new thought movement in a 6:1 ratio. That is what I observed when I attended those types of events, whether it was yoga class or a talk by Dr. Wayne Dyer. Perhaps it is because women are more open to spirit, more attuned to the subtle energies that permeate the planet. Their heightened intuition and awareness is something that I have come to embrace in my own being. Doing so has been so freeing I find it difficult to put words to at times. I am thankful that I have followed their lead and opened myself to a new layer of awareness. This awareness has always been there for me but I was too closed down to honor it. Oh, I felt it. It caused great upheaval in me. But it has taken me years to actually embrace what was occurring inside. I finally started to listen to the call of something that was so much bigger than myself. A call, that once answered, would change my life irreversibly! I am so grateful I opened the door. Albeit it took the universe a while to get through, I love the persistence!

So for me, men's work is about being in balance. The yin and the yang have equal footing in my inside world. It's about embracing the Divine Feminine within myself and honoring that piece of me. As we all honor the Divine Feminine in a deeper, richer, more authentic way, I believe our views will shift. Greed and competition will reduce and love, compassion and understanding will be the new cornerstones. Or perhaps, better yet, they will be revealed as the original cornerstones that were uncovered when we were able to see past the facades of fear, guilt and shame. Having said that, honoring the Divine Masculine also must be embraced equally. For swinging the pendulum too far in any direction will only create the need for a correction.

The Divine Masculine is now in a place of being redefined. Many of us learned about masculinity from heroic archetypes. These archetypes permeate all aspects of our lives and are both worshipped and vilified through our media. In my discernment, the true Divine Masculine is able to wield both hemispheres with conscious awareness and is able to tap into their qualities as he navigates life.

My calling to men's work came to me in late Winter, 2010. I was walking my dogs in the forest one day and pondering whether to attend a course offering called Shift Men's Initiation that showed up in my inbox. The write up was calling for men wishing to step more deeply into their masculinity, to be a leader and be the change they wished to see in the world. It was alluring and fucking terrifying at the same time! I could feel my ego well up as I considered myself to be one of those men I secretly aspired to be. It also picked at my wound of not being good enough and/or worthy. How could I fail…let me count the ways! It was a tough choice. One that I had wrestled with for several weeks before that fateful day in the woods.

As I walked along I was swaying back and forth. Weighing, stepping into something greater with a huge unknown attached to it, against staying safe in a world where I directed the outcome…or so I thought! I stood there looking up at the sun coming through the trees, watching each beam of light leave its warmth on the forest floor. I asked for a sign. In that moment, a hawk swooped down from one of the trees and grabbed a squirrel, stopped for a moment then flew off with the squirrel in its talons! Wow, if that wasn't a sign I don't know what would be!! Instantly, as all this happened, my decision was made. I dropped to my knees with tear-filled gratitude. Another message, this time from my soul thanking me for stepping into the unknown!

I went to this 5-day event and was overwhelmed by the caliber of the men in attendance. The biggest take away for me, at this time, was that I was one of those men. I was one of those men I was putting on a pedestal that had nowhere but down to fall. It was an experience that launched me into men's work in a big way. By the way, that is where I met Michael Taylor and Tom Kelley, two of the men you will hear from in this book.

From that work, I also discovered The ManKind Project. Here was a worldwide organization of men dedicated to the furthering of the mature masculine. Men mentoring men through the passages of their lives. This was the place where I learned to step more fully into my male power while nurturing and embracing the Divine Feminine within. This is where the repressed sides of me started to blossom. And I say repressed "sides" because it was not just the feminine I was repressing but also my authentic masculine. This, I held back, because being clean, clear and authentic with who I was and how I showed up in the world, intimidated other men. It triggered their need to compete. Not because there was something tangible we were vying for, but because their wounds were triggered. The sponsoring thought, again, was I am not good enough and I need to prove to you I am. So I repressed my fullness in order to get the love I so craved. I did not want to cause conflict, because all I wanted was to be loved, accepted and to be worthy to receive that. Sound familiar?

I found that my pain vied for attention through my interactions with others. My wounds would leak out in my words and actions towards others, sometimes leaving impacts that I surely did not intend. But being unconscious to those impacts, as I let my wounds drive the bus, left a wake of hurt and disconnection behind it.

Really stepping in and looking at how I was showing up was a difficult task. The deeper I looked the uglier it seem to get. I saw how I left relationships first so I would not be abandoned. I saw how I would speak louder and sometimes yell if I did not like what the other person was saying. I saw how I manipulated others to get what I wanted. Typically it was attention of some sort. I saw how I numbed myself from myself through eating, television, entertaining, phrases (It's all good) and many other what I consider to be addictions.

Even though I was sitting in a physical circle of men, as I was uncovering shadow after shadow, it was still easy to hide in that group. We were a bunch of lovers who rarely challenged each other. Oh wait, let me reframe that. I challenged others regularly as I hid behind my own offense. What is the saying, the key to a good defense is a good offense…or is it the reverse? Anyway I would regularly get in the face of other men because I could see how they were hiding. That was because I was so fucking good at it myself! If you spot it, you got it! I spiritually bypassed many trying events in my life with words like… it's all good…it was meant to be that way…everything happens for a reason. What those statements did was take me away from the moment and into a fantasy. Mind you there is deep truth in all those words. But when wielded from fear they are just a method of bypassing the feelings and rationalizing the events.

Then an invite came from Graham Phoenix to join the Virtual Men's Gathering. I was intrigued about sitting in a circle of men I did not really know. I did know Michael Taylor and Tom Kelly but only from the first immersion into men's work I mentioned earlier. However, other than that time together three years earlier and some Facebook interactions, I really did not know them.

So there I was sitting in a circle of men from Spain, England, Portugal, Norway, the US and Canada. Wow, how cool was that!! My ego was being boosted by the thought of sitting with all these powerful men. I believed they were all somehow better than I was. All of them were leading men's retreats, writing books and really bringing their gifts to the world! That was the story I told myself. A story that had truth in it, but one that kept me from stepping into my fullness in the group. Again, this reminds me of that saying: it's not the darkness we fear in ourselves but our own light and that if I really showed who I was, I would not be received and would be a fake. A "wannabe" so to speak. Man, was that the farthest thing from the truth! It's amazing what the mind can create when it leans into the feelings of not being good enough…yet again!

As the group unfolded I slowly found my strength. I allowed that strength to rise as I witnessed other men going through similar thoughts of invalidation. Some of the thoughts and beliefs these men, who I judged to be so together, where sharing made mine look so simplistic and invalid. These men, who I had put up on a pedestal, were all just human like me. The difference being that they saw, honored and released the emotions around their wounds. Their wounds were actually beautiful gems in their own crowns of life accomplishments, betrayals, joys, fears and all the messy pieces that make a life lived. Wow, I wanted some of that!!

I slowly learned to release judgments of others and especially myself. Either good or bad judgments. What came through for me was that my judgments of anything were just my unhealed wounds being projected on to others. What I judged was wrong in them was, in fact, what I was covering up about myself.

This was where the gold was. This container of mutual healing that could be accomplished in this faraway online place. As one man did his work he was actually doing my work. This statement is true because we all share similar wounds. In that deep collective space there is something that happens. We enter into a higher consciousness that transcended the typical men's groups I had been part of. The depth of the love could be felt, both in gentle reminders and blessings and the challenges when we feel another man is not showing up fully.

One of the men in my Virtual Men's Group I had a growing affinity for, Eivind, was going through a lot of suffering, learning and releasing as he created his new offering called Reclaim Your Inner Throne. I watched and marveled at his own transformation as he helped others deepen their connections with themselves. After two 12 week rounds went by, I could not stand it anymore! I had to join up! I will not get into details here but what I discovered around the archetypes (Kind, Warrior, Magician, Lover) was astounding. What I unearthed around myself and my abilities was second to none! I really deepened my experience of being here now. Not in the future, not in the past but present with what is. All the energy I spent trying to control, manipulate and/or bring certainly to myself, I could now use in the present moment. That is the pre-sent moment. The moment that, if I stayed present and gave it my all, would be a present to take with me into the future. Talk about a gift! A gift from me to me and one that continues to give to all who I touch. What better way to show that you care about yourself and others than by your presence.

Stop here for just a moment and see where your mind is. Stop reading and let your mind drift. Where does it take you? The kids, the job, the partner. The bills that need to be paid. The dog needs to go in for a checkup. The car's oil is due to be changed. Hundreds if not thousands of possibilities in every moment. Except for where you are at in this moment. Feel your ass on the chair/couch/bed wherever you are. Smell the air. Hear the sounds. What can you do to be more present in this moment. When you read, do your thoughts drift away? Mine do. See if the words on the page can really speak to your soul. Transcend the need to be accomplishing something other than digesting these words. I know when I bring myself into presence, in whatever I am being or doing, the experience is magnified. Don't get me wrong, all of those to-do's are all still there and will get done. But I am not reliving them over and over as I sit across from a beautiful woman at dinner. They do not weigh on me while I am walking my dog along the river. They do not play havoc with me as I lay in bed and step into the place of dreams.

The amount of energy put into the monkey mind is staggering. Bring that energy into the here and now. From this new vantage point watch your life turn into the life that you have dreamt of. Because it does. Your dreams are now your dreams and your reality is one filled with love, compassion and awareness that alchemizes your present into the gift it was meant to be.

Now is the time. The world needs your gifts, the ones that you have been too afraid to share. Your woman needs your gifts of presence and deep love. Your children need a man who keeps his word and shows them what it looks like to be authentic and accountable. Your co-workers and friends desire your fullness of who you are.

When will you trade in your fear for love? When will you heal the wounds that keep you competing, striving and wanting more of whatever it is that you believe you do not have enough of? These are the questions and your answers may change your life irreversibly. Are you ready for that change? Are you ready to be the man you always wanted to be but are too afraid of the impact that may have on yourself and others? I am here to help you step into that space. Let's have a discussion and see if we fit together. It may be the biggest decision of your life.

Tom Kelley

53
Married
Nyack, NY USA

It was the very first men's group I had ever attended. The room was full of American men, most of them white, between 35 and 50 years old. The facilitator looked around at each of us calmly, and said this: "The greatest problem the world today is the American Man."

This is why men's work has become my life's work. I don't want to be part of the problem; I want to be part of the solution.

The facilitator of that group, Tom Monte, went on to become one of my most influential mentors. One of the first things he told me when we began working together was that I was "like a little boy driving a big truck." I was a big strong guy with a solid exterior, always with a serious look on my face. Inside was a sensitive little boy who wanted to be spontaneous and playful—and free. But it was taking everything I had to operate this big piece of machinery called Tom Kelley. This front was not really me.

To me, the goal of Men's Work is to peel back layers of protective armor until you are revealed to yourself and to the world in your most honest and authentic self. Authentic self means that you can feel your emotions, you deal with "what is" and you speak your truth. The protective armor that is blocking this authentic expression in men often takes the form of arrogance, stoicism, heartlessness, violence and dishonesty, just to name a few. Some of the reasons for these blocking strategies is to avoid the vulnerability of:

- Being honest in the face of one's fears
- Admitting hurt or shame from your childhood
- Pain of low self worth
- Fear of being embarrassed
- Afraid of appearing weak or worse ... *feminine*

Another valuable lesson I learned early on was that as men, one of our main jobs in this lifetime is to soften and open. This seems so at odds with what society tells us Men's Work is!

Ahhh ... Men's Work. A loaded phrase. Seen by many as building a deck, or fixing a car, or killing the bat loose in the attic, to others as singing kumbaya around the campfire naked.

I've enjoyed and grown from these types of experiences (and many much weirder). I also consider being on an athletic team or in a military unit as men's work. As a boy and young man, I played on dozens of teams and served in the Marine Corps; two places that the hard edged, stoic "be a man!" culture of manhood ruled. And I thrived there, having been raised that way and not knowing any other way to be.

After leaving the military, I went on to a career in sales. Another bastion of macho (1st place is a Cadillac, 2nd place steak knives, 3rd place YOU'RE FIRED!) culture. It was about 10 years into this phase that things began to shift. Something interesting happened that I now know is quite common. The macho culture kept up with its shallow conversations, kept up its competition by clever put downs, and kept doing all the knuckle-headed things that men do to feel secure in the pack, but I was increasingly out of step. I could still man-up and channel my own inner meathead in situations, but it was creating unease in me. It was also creating stagnation. I got fat, lost my drive, and began asking: is this all there is to life? And is this really me?

This is a point that many men get to. It has many characteristics:

A sense of not belonging to anything.

Lack of enjoying the simple things in life.

Every day seems the same.

He doesn't know how his life got to this point.

And as luck would have it, when I hit 40, my relationship imploded. Note: *I say as luck would have it now, but it took me a while to really see how fortunate I was for the wake-up call.* My long-time girlfriend had seen the light and energy go out of me and found another man who was more alive than me. It was devastating. It was also one of the best things that ever happened to me. She was in India having a great time and I was alone in a big house. I had no idea at the time, but I was embarking on my journey into Men's Work.

Two definitions of Men's Work are:

1. A man dealing with his underlying emotions

2. The practice of coming together as men, with the main intention and focus being to become a better man.

In the examples at the beginning of the chapter, a man's intention is to have a nice deck, a smooth running car, a dead bat and a tingly experience. It is possible for men to grow and learn things about themselves in the process. This is fantastic. In Men's Work with a capital M and W, the main focus is on growth as a man. This growth is almost always INNER growth. I'll go deeper into this because it is so central to the Work. Inner Growth is first and foremost about being able to access feelings and emotions. Without that there is no inner growth. For me, my inner growth path started when my heart was broken. The brokenness allowed me to FEEL my pain. It sucked, but a little part of me knew that if I could feel my pain then it followed that maybe I could feel more joy and love. Turns out the shield was blocking my pain from being felt but also blocking love from going outward or inward. This shield that many men put up is encouraged by our societal image of what masculinity is and also our upbringing. From a young age, boys are taught that the term "be a man" means to always have your guard up, don't show any emotions except anger, and never appear vulnerable. This style of thinking has evolved over the years. Hollywood's 50's and 60's tough guys have morphed into slightly more multi-dimensional characters. But the core message remains: real men still don't eat quiche. Our society and culture often does not encourage boys and men to ever stop and feel; to look inside themselves and ask the questions: What do I want? Do my needs matter? What is my purpose? This has resulted in generations of men out of touch with their feelings and their power with no way to articulate why they are frustrated and drifting through life. So how does this kind of *Men's Work* facilitate and create space for vulnerability? This is where men's groups like the Virtual Men Group come in. One way for men to reconnect with themselves and learn to cultivate their vulnerability is to form a regular meeting circle with other men. A group size ranging from 5 to 16 men works well. The group should be large enough to shift the focus off the individual but not have too many members. It's important that every man gets an opportunity to speak. In order for most men to be comfortable enough to discuss issues that previously have been off limits, the right environment must be created. One of the first ways to do this is to set up firm ground rules around how the group interacts. Certain upfront agreements are crucial to building the trust necessary to go to a deeper level of communication. The first rule is no talking over, or cutting someone off, when they are speaking. Notice how common this is the next time you are in a group of men. It is the main form of communication in bars, golf courses and workplaces. Its absence in a men's group encourages a free flow of authentic feelings to surface, which starts the process of reconnecting to our power. All men also must agree that all things talked about in the circle are confidential. When this trust is established, the men are much more likely to go deeper into themselves. Another aspect of a highly functioning men's group is avoiding trying to "fix" the person or his problem. Rather, evoke from him the truth that he already knows but is feeling blocked from being able to do anything about. This is done by asking questions or offering new perspectives on the issue. In time, these techniques create a supportive, non-judgmental setting. It becomes a place where real breakthroughs can happen and men can feel what they feel. I have seen this format work wonders in so many different settings and with so many different types of men over the last 13 years. That first men's group that I attended was in 2003 at a macrobiotics institute. I have sat in a circle with men on a mountaintop at a Zen Buddhist retreat center in Crestone, Colorado with one of David Deida's mentors. I've attended many David Deida's workshops at retreat centers and in NYC conference rooms. I've led Manly Awareness workshops in medium and maximum security prisons, including the infamous Sing Sing prison and even in the Virtual Men's Gatherings that have come into being with the improvements in video technology I have been amazed at how certain elements are always present.

The Circle - Or the square boxes on video calls. Whether it is in person in a circle or in evenly sized boxes on a screen, everyone can see one another and everyone has each other's back (or in other words, no one has their back to anyone else). No hierarchy. Sitting on the ground in the circle is also common, further leveling the playing field.

The Grounding - At many men's groups, men are coming from different places and situations in their day and the initial energy is very chaotic. The Grounding is a way to get in the same vibration and calm the chaotic energy. The grounding can take the form of chanting together or one of the men talking the others through a guided meditation. The closing of eyes alone is very grounding and unifies energy well.

The Talking Stick - The talking stick is a traditional device used by groups to organize and civilize talking at gatherings. When a man has the stick (usually in his check in; we will get to that next), he has the floor. He can't be interrupted and gets to speak his mind until he's done. The talking stick gives men the unique chance to speak for a bit of time with no chance of being interrupted. This is YOUR time to tell your story and your truth. Try finding a conversation in a bar where dudes let another one finish his story, let alone his sentence.

The Check in - Men are encouraged to check in with how they are feeling right in the moment. Other check ins can be about how their life has gone since the last meeting. The important thing is for the men to tell their own stories and really get in touch with and share what they are going through. Why is this important? Because these men may not have ANY other place to open up and tell their story. At work they have to look competent. At home they have to "have it together," at the bar with their friends they have to be tough or smart or any other way they think that they "have" to be. But at a men's group, they can just be who and how they really are—dropping the mask and showing vulnerability.

Vulnerability is the pathway to the type of freedom that many men are looking for—the freedom that they don't have in dead marriages and boring, meaningless jobs. Many middle-aged men wake up one day in their 30s or 40s and realize they have no close friends, no one to tell their inner thoughts to, and no joy in life. This is rough. To wake up in middle age and realize that the blueprint to "success" and the path to a good life wasn't accurate. Worse, it was a ruse. That is brutal. So many men's groups are the first time men have heard other men open up about their own challenges in such a way. It is so liberating to know that we are not alone.

The Virtual Men's Gathering was a little different in that we came together with the understanding that all the men in the group had done some men's work before and were involved in the "men's work" field in some capacity. I have been coaching men and leading in-person and virtual groups and programs for men since 2010. I was drawn to the VMG as a way to broaden my circle of men. And the group that Graham drew together was amazingly broad with men from all over Europe and North America. It really opened my eyes to how little is lost on a video call compared to in person. The only thing lacking that takes away from the rawness and the experience is touch: no hugs or no use of pushing or physical exchanges to deepen exercises. But the rest of the magic remains surprisingly powerful.

I met three of the men who wrote chapters in this book at the 2011 Shift Men's Initiation in California. Then, when Graham formed this group a few years later, Michael Taylor and Richard Arsic were on the initial call. I remember thinking "I remember these guys," which gave me a feeling of connection and belonging. We had been doing the bi-weekly VMG calls for over two years when Richard and I went back to California to staff another men's workshop named the Sword and Scepter. Richard and I got there the day before the workshop and when he picked me up in his truck it was strange to see him—for about 5 seconds. Then I realized that I really knew him and that we had become friends on an extremely deep level without seeing each other in person for years. Point is, you don't lose that much in the video format. That is one of the side benefits of all the types of men's groups: while I was peeling back my layers and developing as a man, I was forging some of the deepest and most meaningful friendships in my life. No small thing indeed.

One of the other big benefits of Men's work is that it trains men to be mentors. I believe that society would be completely transformed if every man over 30 years old were to mentor another man.

First, let's define some terms: Role model vs. mentor.

Years ago, Charles Barkley famously declared that he didn't want to be considered a role model. As a young man he would get into hot water for spitting on fans and throwing tantrums and so naturally he didn't want to be responsible for others mimicking that behavior. But did he really have a choice? Aren't you a role model just by being in a role?

Take fatherhood. If you are a boy and you have a father, then he is modeling the role of father, especially for you. There is no choice in the matter. If he has integrity and good character, then that's what fatherhood looks like to you. If he is absent and always angry, then that is what the role of father looks like to you.

When men get into their 30s, 40s, and 50s they are modeling the role of being an adult man to all younger men. Not enough adult men seem to conscious of this. I'll never forget when a thirty year old man came to his first men's group and said, "I just wanted to find older men who weren't all shut down, guarded, and negative." He was actively looking around for POSITIVE role models and couldn't find any.

So the first step in this societal transformation is for men to be willing to do the inner work to improve themselves. Then any improvement—any more tolerance, any more calm eye contact during conversations, and more non-judgmental ways of looking at things—would be on display for all the men coming down the path.

The second step is the one that would really tip the scales. This is where mentoring comes in.

The dictionary defines mentoring as:

1. a wise and trusted counselor or teacher.

2. an influential senior sponsor or supporter.

So being a mentor can also be looked at as ACTIVELY being a positive role model to ANOTHER. To consciously take a break from our own concerns and train our attention on what someone else is going through. Eye contact, active listening, patience…all of it. They are the focus for this period of time. When you are in the mentoring mode and someone is spending time with you, that person is spending time with YOU! You get their full attention. If someone says something to you from the side you do not get distracted. It's presence. And it's an honoring of the conversation and the moment, which also means you can't BS or hide. The moment gets very real.

This is why I believe that this is powerful enough to transform society and the world, because it's exponential. One mentor can mentor many. Then they mentor many. And eventually everyone is getting real.

And that concept of exponential influence is one of the lasting legacies of VMG for me. The magic of modern technology allows 10 men from all over the world to come together in wildly different time zones for a common cause: to become better men so we can help other men become better men. This is why I started Open Deep and True (opendeepandtrue.com). I love what has happened in my life because of Men's Work. I have a fantastic wife, a great love life, a precious daughter and many interesting and *up to something* friends. My life is filled with wonder and I even know when I am full of shit most of the time. I want that for other men.

I know that **it happens at the point of connection.** Men have to show up, they have to get past the brief discomfort that comes with trying something new. Open Deep and True is going to continue to offer one-on-one coaching, men's groups, and unique training programs and will increasingly offer virtual opportunities (online video meetings) for boys and men. All avenues for them to connect, deepen and flourish, exponentially.

I'll end my chapter with a common term in Men's Groups that for me means, *I feel the connection.*

Aho!

Enric Carbó

53
Divorced
Tortosa, Catalonia (Spain)

Why do you believe men's work is important?

I believe men's work is extremely important because our world has changed a lot and we don't have a clear model of what is to be a man and what it should be. There is a situation of uncertainty because the old models have died out. Adding to it, our culture, both pop and academic, usually has an underlying message that more or less says, *"Men don't have problems, men are the problem,"* insisting on what men shouldn't be instead of working out with positive models and roles.

The future is not written, neither the present, and even the past can be re-written in the light of new discoveries. Who can say what is a man, what it should be? Only through work can we discover it, only marching on our way of being a man can we find it out by ourselves. This is a group task, alone we will not go far.

We all have our conditioning: biological as a species, cultural for being at the beginning of 21st century, biographical for being nourished by our mum and dad (or lack of them…). Conditioning is just a part of ourselves, we cannot deny it, but we can transcend it and go beyond it. We can and we must widen our limits, but we can only do it when we are aware of them. We mainly get aware of our limits by relating with others then our conditioning shows up. Without any work on ourselves, we usually relate *from* our conditioning. When you are in a group of men and you listen to your companions, when you attune to their experience, their life with its ups and downs, you get a reflection of yourself that enables you to be more aware of your conditioning and also be more aware of new opportunities and challenges that open in your life. Then you learn to relate *through* your conditioning instead *from* it. This demands honest feedback from your companions and a sustainable practice of authenticity.

It is not easy to practice authenticity as men. We have been taught to go to the world with the mask of invulnerability, and we hide behind it, not only from the others but specially from ourselves, until we forget who really we are—what our my real needs are and where our souls are To have friends, or a spouse, or to belong to a spiritual community are important for the life and evolution of any man. There we may actualize our highest potential. Any of those relationships can be the most significant in our lives, where we can find meaning. On the other side, how are we living those relationships? Are we authentic to our friends or our partner? Are we really authentic to ourselves relating to them? Here is where a men's group is doing its job. It is not a substitute for the most significant relationships we build thorough our life, but it is a strong complement that helps us to face our real self, and it challenges us to live our highest potential in our relationships. And as I said, this job of facing our real self and its challenges is not a job that can be done individually.

How did you first become involved with men's work?

By 2005, I was in a personal growth group called "Escola de Vida" (School of Life) in Barcelona. We used to meet in a beautiful house in the mountains called Can Benet Vives. There we held workshops and other spiritual practices with an anthropologist called Josep Mª Fericgla. He applied Jungian psychology and Sufi spiritual practices in his work. He was mainly a specialist in shamanism and expanded states of consciousness. He had been with Shuar (Jivaro) Indians in Ecuador's Amazonia, learned from shamans and wrote some books about them and how they use entheogens in their culture.

In this context of self-growth and self discovery, we decided to meet in order to deepen our practices and our relationship, so we started with regular meetings every month. We had already become friends as we all belonged to the "Escola de Vida", but we were not a mere group of male friends who meet one Friday evening a month to share a meal and have a good time together—even though we did that too.

So my first involvement with a men's group was a mixture of friendship and commitment to a group in order to grow. I know that friendship is not strictly necessary for getting involved in men's group work, that what it is necessary is a commitment to oneself and to the group to be authentic and honest, but this is how we started and it worked well. One by one, through time, we all left the "Escola de Vida" due to our personal evolution that brought us to different paths. Nevertheless, we have maintained our group and our meetings, and we still meet regularly ten years later.

Later on, realizing the benefits of my membership to this men's group, I decided to create and lead a men's group in the city where I live. It hasn't been an easy task, but the job done has been highly rewarding. I live in a small city in a conservative area where most men honestly live according to traditional values. When they hear about a group of men who gather together in order to talk, and not about football, cars or women, but about themselves and how are they living their lives, they frown, finding it odd, having the suspicion that it may be a cult or something rare. Nevertheless, we have kept our group for four years and it is still running.

What is different about you as a result of doing men's work? What have you learned about yourself?

My first impression to answer this is that I have gained more presence. I know I have a space where I can share feelings, thoughts and challenges that are not easy to share anywhere else in this manner. Of course I have relationships with friends, partners and family where I share many things. Anyway, with those relationships, often my way of relating is crystallized by habits, a sort of "automatic pilot". The power of habit weakens when I am in my men's group, so presence strengthens.

Another thing I can see in myself is that I have gained more autonomy, especially in my relations with women. Until I was involved with men's work I hadn't experienced much intimacy with men. I always have had male friends, and some good friends. But I usually had the experience of intimacy, specifically to be able to be open to my own emotions, with women. Women were very important to me, may be too much. Now I have realized that I was looking for something with women that I should give to myself. I used them as a sort of gate to access some parts of myself that I was unwilling to acknowledge. Writing like this, it would seem that I disdain women more than before I got involved with men's work, but it is the other way round. This is because I have experienced this authentic intimacy that emerges in men's group work, and now I feel more rooted in myself so I am more aware of the polarity that is created within the relationship between a man and a woman. This authenticity to myself has helped me a lot to be also authentic with my relationships with women. I no longer need to play the role of the "nice man" (quite inauthentic) in order to seek for their approval. Relationships in general are a source of challenges, but are also the way to a fulfilled life. Since I have become involved with men's groups, my relationships, especially with women, have improved a lot. It is not only my opinion, this is also what most of my female friends say.

I have also learned to be more open with my vulnerability and my shortcomings because I have witnessed other men in the group to be bold enough to share their vulnerability and their shortcomings.

As I said before, our conditioning as men is to hide behind a mask of invulnerability. In my case, I told myself stories like *"I am not like them..."* to pretend that I am different. In other words, to disconnect from the parts of myself I don't like. I could deny my pain by telling the well-known story of *"I am fine; everything is Ok"*, or sometimes the other way round: *"Nobody can imagine what I am going through, I cannot explain it to anyone"*. The summary of this unbalanced perspective about myself would be *"nobody is like me"*, because I would deny my pain or I would internalize it so it occupied all the space, which is also a subtle form of escaping from myself. When I am in a men's group, practicing authenticity, and I hear a companion sharing a part of himself, exposing himself to the group, I start realizing that my fears, my shame, my hopes, my anger are not unique to me, or I can also realize that he is a mirror where I can see the fear and the shame I have denied in myself pretending that *"I am fine"*. Of course, his story or his issues are not mine, but he is a mirror where my hidden issues can emerge and then I can take notice of them. This is a great help to start being in contact with these ugly parts of myself that I don't like to witness, and I can do it in a *safe environment*. Sooner or later, life puts us in situations where we have to face our own stuff. The more we escape from ourselves, the more traumatic it can be when this day arrives that we have to meet with those parts that we haven't taken care of. To have this sacred space, where I can be myself, because other men are themselves, and where we share this commitment to be authentic and also compassionate, has been a space to grow, to learn to enter those aspects of myself that are painful, a little bit more in every meeting. It is not an easy task, sometimes I shut myself down, or I would get angry. But when we have created that safe environment, and the commitment is alive, this is also part of the work, and can be dealt within the group, so finally it also becomes a source of learning and growing.

What are the benefits you have received from participating in the Virtual Men's Gathering?

One of the benefits, in my particular case, is to practice English. I know this has nothing to do with men's work, but it has been an extra benefit. English is not my mother tongue, I live in Catalonia so my current languages are Catalan and Spanish. To be fluent in another language demands practice, so it has been an opportunity and a challenge to be in the Virtual Men's Gathering. It has been a challenge because it has demanded me to be very present and attuned, and even with that, sometimes I miss parts of the conversation, especially when jokes are involved. I can see all the men bursting out laughing and I miss the point… luckily this happens only from time to time.

The main benefit has been to be with men who are already working in men's groups. To me, this has been an extraordinary learning to share with them. The level of commitment and respect is very deep. I can see real men sharing real emotions, sharing their truth, and I am with them trying to share mine. This commitment is shown because we usually speak in first person, we don't talk about the world, trying to "fix" it, or talk about you and what you said. It is not as easy as it seems to speak mainly about myself, of what I really think, of what I feel; there is an easy way to escape from opening oneself by going to the second person talking about what someone else said, or giving advise instead of feedback, or going to the third person talking about the people or the world. This practice has been a great learning to me.

Another benefit has been the creativity shown in the group. I considered myself a sort of *amateur* in men's groups. Now I am with some men who make their living coaching and working with men, so they are continuously facing new challenges and creating for that job. They share it within the group and I have learned a lot from them.

It has been also a new experience to me to be in a Virtual Gathering; in fact, it has been a new experience to all of us. When we met the first time, we didn't know very well how it was going to function. I think due to the previous work we all had before the virtual meeting, we quickly "entered" into the job. It has also helped our private group on Facebook where we can share other things between meetings.

What I can say, after these two years, is that I count on my group. I have been able to share my joys and also my difficulties in my life. I know I will be heard, and I will also receive precious feedback. Now, when I go through challenges, I know I can count on my group. I often wait for our meeting on Fridays in order to share something personal that I know I can share with confidence with my companions. And when I do not have anything so important to share, I am also looking forward to our next meeting because other men will share something that will concern me. It's amazing to have achieved this level of confidence with men from different parts of the world where the only way we can see and talk to each other is through video conferencing. Now I have used videoconferences for other issues also with confidence thanks to what I have learned in the Virtual Men's Gathering.

What is your vision and passion for the future of men?

After my experience with men's groups, I have become more and more passionate about this task of working on our masculinity together in order to evolve as human beings. We only became men among other men. I never really thought very much about my masculinity until I started with this men's work ten years ago. To me, to be a man was just to be a man, and that was all; I sympathized with most feminist theses, and I tried to be a conscious, sensitive man, as demanded by the culture of politically correctness in which I was moving. Now, my experience of sharing with other men, as I said above, has given me such presence, depth and authenticity, and also has shown me my self-deceits and shortcomings in an environment that is both loving and rigorous, so that I want to spread such an enriching experience.

We have come to this existence just as human beings, but our form of human being is as men. Yes, to be a man is something given, but it is also something that we can work on, expand and deepen. And now I know that this is a task to be done in a group setting. That's why I created a men's group in the city where I am living. The slogan of our group is *"we explore our masculinity and how to evolve to our purpose together"*. To work the life's purpose is something developed in many schools and many groups. I think it is beautiful work necessary to find meaning and grounding. We all have gifts to offer to the world, whatever our form or our condition. As men, we have great gifts to offer. The world needs a healthy masculinity, especially in our culture where masculinity is a little shaky. As I said at the beginning, old models are dying out and do not serve the purpose that the world is demanding of us as men anymore, and the evolution to our highest expression is something that we have to work out.

My vision is that those spaces, where men gather together in order to see each other, to learn, to evolve and to practice authenticity, will grow and multiply. These sacred spaces are devoted to us not hiding ourselves or avoiding risks, or to develop unhealthy male competitiveness, but to gain strength and commitment to our highest purpose, to work in groups to the best expression of what we can become. These groups can take many forms: social, spiritual, political groups of men. I know some already exist. My vision is that those groups of men will have a "plus" of awareness of the gift of masculinity and the commitment that it demands to return this gift to the world in a healthy way. There is no a unique form to do that, as there is not a unique form of being a man. There are healthy and unhealthy forms of masculinity. To evolve towards the healthiest form is a group task, where voices of men and women must be heard, but this evolutionary job of masculinity in group must be done by men with other men. I am happy and proud to be on this path.

Graham Reid Phoenix

69
Married
Spain

My Relationship with Men and Groups of Men

When I was young, I always felt that I was shy. I found it difficult to connect with and talk to people. I would avoid situations where I had to have a conversation with someone I did not know.

I felt that this came from my relationship with my family, in particular with my father and my two brothers. I was the youngest of three boys and they always made sure I knew who was at the bottom. My eldest brother seemed to get great enjoyment out of teasing me to the point where I would get angry and shout or hit back. This was usually when my mother came on the scene, ensuring that I was the one who got into trouble. Although we now have a great relationship, we did not then. My father was, in my eyes, the cause of all the strife between us brothers. He was a dominant man, kind but dominating. He always had to have the last word on everything. This frustrated the hell out of us boys and made us determined to win wherever we could. This meant that we tried to be this way with each other. Strife, anger and fighting was the result.

This created in me the need to win all the time. I always needed to have the last word. I hated others putting me down or showing me to be in the wrong, even when I was. This made me a determined and difficult man, especially with other men. My relationships with men were always a challenge. I needed people to recognize me. I wanted them to acknowledge me for who I was. I wanted them to see what I had done.

This became obvious when I started to work in the theatre. I was a stage manager, electrician and then a lighting designer. I was in a new and strange world where I found it difficult to connect with people, with other men. I needed to establish who I was and I chose to do it through the use of physical power. This was not a clever thing to do.

There was one occasion early on when I was just nineteen. I had started work in a new theatre and I was in charge of the temporary stage crew. These were volunteers from the local town who had been working in the theatre for years. On one occasion, I was trying to organize them and tell them what to do. They were messing around and not being serious about what I was saying. I became frustrated and my anger blew up. I hit one guy in the stomach to get his attention. It worked then but I did not build rapport with them.

After that moment, I tended to use subtler means to get my way. I became good at persuasion, at being able convince people that I was right. This was the crux of the matter. I always had to be right.

It is interesting that my relationships with women did not have the same edge to it. I was even more shy when it came to dating. I found it impossible to think that I would be attractive to women in any way. As long as this issue was out of the way, though, I was on solid ground. I found a great affinity with women when I worked in the theatre. I could talk to them, relate to them and not feel challenged by them.

When I came to my first major relationship, I found the courage to persuade her to be with me. I created what, at first, was a great relationship. Later, after we married, I started to find a courage that overcame my shyness. I became more certain in myself. I found a sense of certainty that was separate from my desire to dominate.

I fathered two boys, continuing the male dominance in my family. My desire to dominate crept back and often interfered in our relationships. To some extent, they learned the same tendency to anger that I had learned from my father. It was just so easy for me to go there without realizing what was happening.

Running a business, a lighting design consultancy, put me up against other men, on the whole. The world I worked in was male dominated, as are many working worlds. My desire to dominate had free reign and I became a great success.

I became good at organizing and getting people to do things. This applied to my working world and the volunteer worlds I occupied. I often became the chairman of any committee I joined and used my persuasive skills to get people moving. I found that this was a great way of being in groups, especially of men. This happened without the need to connect to them on a personal level. I was able to be in there without actually being in there, if you see what I mean. I could be quite charismatic in these situations because I loved people looking up to me. I loved people listening to me.

I became aware of the difficulties of this type of situation. This happened during the period when I was an evangelical Christian. I found that I had to expose myself and get to know people on a deeper level. The scary bit was getting to know other men on a deep and personal level. Organizing and doing work was one thing, but in this setting, that was not enough. People wanted you to join in. I became involved because I wanted to join in, at last. I no longer liked of being on the sidelines pretending that I was important.

I joined a Men's Group at my church and started to relate more to other men. This was a difficult experience for me. The focus was on conforming to their accepted lifestyle. I found that I did not fit in to what they expected. My wife was not a churchgoer and they found it difficult to understand why we did not come to church as a family. They were big on family and they spent time trying to help me fix this situation. That was not what I was there for.

Much later, I fixed this particular situation by leaving my wife and my marriage. We had been together for about 35 years and our boys were now grown up. Looking back, I suppose that I had jumped into marriage too early. From my upbringing I believed that marriage was a commitment you made for life. It was long time after I realized it was not working and I built up the courage to call it a day.

After I left and, for the first time in my life, lived in a flat on my own, I found myself completely out of my depth. I had spent so many years in one relationship that I did not know how to go about relating to women, this time. Here I am, not talking about friends but about relationships. I had no idea how to go about being with a woman let alone how to create a relationship.

I met a woman and we related well to each other and I slipped in to my persuasive mode and got pushed back. It seemed that this was not the way to go about it. I lost my ability to deal with this without the main tool I had used to get through life in one piece. She could make her own mind up and did not need me to tell her what she should do with her life. The other aspect that came to the fore was the lack of an electric charge between us. I realized that sexual polarity was important for creating a powerful relationship. Between a man and a woman, it creates a strong bond. This was just not present and I did not understand why.

We ended up having a conversation by text between Britain and America. I was trying to build a relationship between us and she was on the verge of walking away. I realized later that she was trying to encourage me to be a man and find my inner strength and courage.

This is the issue that goes right back to when I was young. I strove to understand what she was trying to say to me and kept failing.

At the end of the conversation, I finally realized that I just had to become a man for myself. It was important to let go of the idea of the relationship. I needed to get in touch with my own inner masculinity and my courage as a man. It was about me not about anyone else. This was nothing to do with how I related to anyone else. It was nothing to do with people liking me or me impressing people. It was just about me being me and trusting that that was not only alright but that it was also amazing.

She told me that when I got back to Britain I had completely changed. I had turned into the man she always knew I could be and the kind of man she could be with. This excited and scared her. She questioned whether I would stay there, whether I was serious about who I had become. She realized that I was staying there and that I was deepening my relationship with myself. This became scary for her.

We ended up becoming intimate. We built a relationship with a deep polarity and intimacy. We are now married and our relationship grows day by day, ever improving. Having made this discovery about myself I was able to start letting go of trying to be someone for other people. I had found a way of being myself and enjoying every moment of it. This was a revelation for me, just to be myself with all my inner masculine power and strength.

I was so excited by this shift and so amazed by the results that came from it that I began to write about it. I developed a website called 'MaleXperience' (it is now at 'grahamreidphoenix.com'). In it, I wrote about being a man and finding my masculinity. The more I looked around me, the more I saw men in desperate need to connect with themselves. They were looking to find their own inner manhood. I saw that there had been too much emphasis on achievement and results, both in business and in dating women. It all seemed to be about what you could do to get the results. It was about how you could create an outer persona which would bring others along with you. This reminded me so much of my earlier life. I had cut myself off from people by pretending and wearing a mask of masculinity.

I reached out with my writing and connected with other men. These men were either finding their own answers or were looking for their own answers. I was able to open up my experience for people to learn from and start coaching people in how to move forward. I started talking to people in the world of men's work and learning more about the bigger world of men out there.

I started connecting with men.

I continued with the Personal Development work that I had been pursuing for many years. I had been to some events put on by Tony Robbins. There I had learned a great deal about growing myself and helping other people. I became a volunteer at his events. There I turned my ability to organize people into an ability to relate to people, men and women.

I also did some work with Christopher Howard and was able to spend some time with him in Venice over a few days. We used the time to record some conversations about men and masculinity. This was an amazing experience. We spent time every day talking about being men, or not being men. We explored our individual approaches to masculinity. This was the first time I had talked to someone with such intensity about this. It was the first time I had been so open with another man about these issues. The result was so powerful that I wrote a book from the conversations that I published on Kindle. It still has an impact for men today.

Later I moved on from this experience to start my own radio show called 'Men Alive'. The idea was to take this idea and explore it with other men, men of all types. I recorded about 25 shows with men. I explored who they were and talked about their approach to masculinity. The year I did this was an exciting period of my life. It was a period that enabled me to grow my own ideas of masculinity even further.

My new found ability to relate to other men underpinned my working and volunteer worlds. This applied even outside men's work. There was a key event that expanded my awareness. It was a conference called 'The Evolving Men's Conference', held in Boulder, Colorado. It brought together men for men's work from both sides of the Atlantic. It tried to steer a common path for us to develop, but in many ways it was not a success. None of the ideas or programs we discussed came to anything and no work continued from it. What did work for me was my ability to get close to other men. For a long weekend we sat in a large circle and opened ourselves up to what was there for us. This involved honesty and authenticity, something I was not used to with men.

From there I developed my writing and coaching. I started creating online courses for men. I found it difficult, though, because I was back in Spain, where I live, isolated from the kind of men I had come to enjoy relating to. Many of these men followed me on Facebook and read my blog, but this was too distant a relationship to help me. Many of these men were in men's circles. They, on a weekly basis, sat with each other and explored the depths of their souls. I had never had this on a regular basis with other men and it was something I longed for.

One day, I gathered up my courage and started something which altered my life. It set in motion ripples that are still going today.

I put a post out on Facebook asking for men who wanted to start a virtual men's group. I called it a 'Virtual Men's Gathering'. I had researched this online hoping to find one that I could join with no success. I decided that there was no other option than to start one myself.

I got some responses to my request both from men I knew and ones I did not. I gathered them together and created a group that still meets three years later. We meet every two weeks at the same time and we support each other and delve into each other's issues. We fight and argue and laugh together.

For me, the transformation has been enormous. The only regret I have is that I did not start one a lot earlier. The existence of technology that allowed us to meet online and look into each other's eyes was a great help. I think that there was a merging of the idea of meeting across the world. There was a desire to open out men's work to be more available and more accessible for all men.

I get upset and frustrated in the group from time to time and I get uplifted and inspired. The other men often push my buttons and I push theirs. The group does not get rid of these issues but it enables us to work through them and stop them ruling our lives.

Every other Friday at 7:00pm in Spain, I have a get-together that is top priority. I spend the time relaxing and being present with the other men who join that evening. I explore what I feel and I explore what other men are feeling. Men join from their cars, from cafes and, in one memorable incident, from their hospital bed.

I cannot emphasize enough to all men reading this that belonging to a men's group is an essential to being a man. Many can join a face-to-face group in their area, but for many, like me, these just do not exist. Either find an existing virtual group or do what I did and start your own. The technology is easy and the benefits are enormous.

I have found that men have difficulties connecting with other men on a deep or spiritual basis. I practice Yoga on a regular basis and all the classes I attend are with women. I attended one men's class which limped along for a year and then died out. I would love to encourage men to not see this as something week or feminine. It is the greatest work that a man can do. It has taken most of my life for me to get to this point of deep connection, it does not have to take as long for you.

Brett Churnin

44
Married
Sydney, Australia

Why do you believe Men's Work is important?

If our desire is to create healthy and harmonious relationships with ourselves and with those around us, then we all need to do some work—men and women alike. Men can learn a lot from women, and it is valuable for men and women to do some of that work together, but it is equally important for some of that work to be done separately.

Men's work is important because most men are confused about what 'being a man' means in today's world. How does a 'good man' act? What are the characteristics of a 'real man'? What are the essential 'masculine' qualities? How is 'manhood' attained? And whilst there is no 'one' definitive answer to these questions, we need to get more clarity on what the answers are for each of us.

In part, we lack this clarity because most of us learned from fathers and male role models who portrayed an image of masculinity that was founded in antiquated ideals and characteristics. They held to a belief that being vulnerable or expressing emotion is a sign of weakness; that a man's role is to provide and his success in life is defined by financial or business acumen; and that the path to manhood is paved by the conquest of others.

In realizing that we were losing others trying to maintain this 'man up' tough veneer, we went to the other extreme and then lost ourselves trying to be 'sensitive new-age' men. Men's Work is important because we need to find a new balance; we need to find a new way of being as men. We need to find softness with our strength, yet stay grounded and centered with our sensitivity. We need to re-connect with our true purpose and mission, and we need to re-learn how to communicate openly and authentically.

Men's work is not just important, it is essential. Take a look at the statistics on depression and suicide, homicide and domestic violence, and the numbers don't look good for men. Something has to change, and Men's Work is essential to creating that change.

How did you first become involved with Men's Work?

When I first realized that in order to change and impact my external world I had to do some work on my inner world, the intuitive path initially was for me to reflect and introspect on my own. So I did a lot of intense meditation. I did four 10-day Vipassana courses (each one 10 days of sitting in silence), plus a myriad of other meditation retreats. And whilst this path had its merits, it was also limited—I realized that there was only so much that I could see from my own perspective.

So the next logical path was to seek outside guidance, and that involved some intense 1-1 work with a variety of professionals. This was powerful work for me as a man because others could see aspects of myself that I was unaware of. They could help reveal things about myself that I didn't even know I didn't know. The more I realized the impact and importance of feedback from others, the more open I was to receiving it, and the more I sought.

But my true immersion into real men's work was in 2004 when I completed an 8-week intensive course with seven other men called 'Trusting the Masculine'. I learned a load about myself over those 8 weeks but the greatest gift from the course came with the realization of the value and worth of guidance from other men and **group work with other men**. Soon after, I started my own regular Men's Group with a few friends and, 10 years later, it is still the most important men's work I do. I cannot imagine living as powerfully or peacefully without it.

What is different about you as a result of doing men's work?

Growing up, I found it difficult to connect with other boys. I was looking for real friendships, and it seemed easier to do so with girls than boys, so most of my closest friends were girls. As a young man, I still yearned for honest and open connections with other men, beyond chats about sport or women or work. There always seemed to be an element of separation, competition or superficiality. Starting a men's group was my stand for something greater, deeper and more meaningful between men.

Men's Group has changed the way I relate to myself as a man and how I relate to other men.

It solidified my belief that men <u>can</u> find a place and space with each other that is supportive, respectful and caring. It opened my eyes to the struggle that all men endure when we suppress our fears and the stress and strain we experience when we try to maintain a stoic exterior that exudes "I've got it all handled" when we really don't.

Men's group has demanded me to be accountable and responsible for my actions.

Through my men's group I have developed a level of integrity that is now essential to my strength, power and confidence. I now trust myself as a man who honors his word and cleans the shit up when I can't fulfill on what I said I could.

Men's group has demanded me to understand and manage my own emotions.

The space we have created is safe and what goes on in men's group stays in men's group. That space has enabled me to freely express and explore every emotion on the scale—whether it is intense anger, dark shame or pure joy. The ability to do so has transformed how I relate to and manage my emotions on a daily basis in my everyday life.

Men's group has demanded me to find a balance between backbone and heart.

Before men's group, I was comfortable expressing my 'softer' and gentler side, but found it challenging to embrace my strength and power. I know for many men it's the other way around, but regardless, I think most men are challenged to find a balance between the two. Men's group enabled me to find this balance and to identify those times when I need to re-calibrate.

Men's group has demanded me to communicate openly, authentically and powerfully.

Every two weeks I get an opportunity to speak my truth, to listen to others and to give others feedback. These are skills that every man can learn and develop and have made a huge difference to the way I communicate in my personal and professional worlds.

Men's group has demanded me to live a life I love, one that reflects my values and beliefs.

Men's group has helped me to have a better grasp on who I am, what's important to me, and how I relate to myself and the world around me. The men in my group have come to understand what I'm committed to and how I want to live my life, and they're a constant reminder for me to be the grandest vision of my greatest self.

What have you learned about yourself?

I have learned that 'the work' I need to do is constant and never-ending.

In seeing and accepting my capacity for greatness and darkness, I have learned to embrace my humanity.

I have learned that my capacity to succeed in life is only limited by my beliefs.

I have learned how to be generous—generous in my listening to other men, generous in my contribution to other men, and generous with myself.

I have learned that my vulnerability is a strength, not a weakness.

I have learned that I can be ruthless and I can be compassionate, but to be ruthlessly compassionate is an ongoing learning process.

What is your vision and passion for the future of men?

Over the years of being involved in a Men's Group, the benefits to me and the other men were so palpable. It became clear to me that men's groups are one of the most powerful vehicles for men's work and I wanted other men to experience what we'd experienced. I wanted to take the mystery out of what Men's Groups are and I wanted to make Men's Groups more accessible to all men.

Together with my fellow Men's Group brother and best mate Mike Britton, we created the Men's Group Field Guide. It's a free, step-by-step guide on how to set up and sustain an effective Men's Group. It's not the bible—there are many forms and formats for running a Men's Group but it details what has worked for us and many other groups over the years.

Since we launched it in 2012, over 700 men from all over the world have requested a copy of the guide through our website, www.mensgroup.info. Many of those men have since started up their own group. Some contacted us from existing groups needing to refine and refresh their process and some just wanted to join an existing group. It was clear that there were already many groups running that no one knew about and many men who wanted to get involved. So that led us to set up www.mensgroupdirectory.com, a global men's group directory designed to be the go-to website to connect men with existing men's groups.

Men's Groups: what women want and men need

At a dinner party last year, I mentioned to the couple sitting next to me that I'd been involved in a Men's Group for years and was passionate about helping other men to get involved. "I'd LOVE my husband to get involved in a Men's Group," she exclaimed, giving him a nudge. "No chance in hell…" was his immediate reply.

I was fascinated that his wife was so eager for him to give it a go, yet he was so resistant. Together that night, we explored where that resistance might come from and why men's groups are what women want (for their men) and what men need.

Firstly, it may be because talking openly and honestly with other men doesn't come naturally to most men, unless of course we've had a few drinks. Then the truth may come out but it's rarely a powerful conversation, nor one that leaves any lasting impact. Women want their men to be better communicators, yet many men struggle to express themselves when it really counts. In the right environment (like in a Men's Group), communication is a skill that men can learn and develop.

Secondly, many men have a fear of being vulnerable or emotional, especially in the presence of other men. It goes against the grain of what many men think (or have been taught) masculinity is about. But women want to feel that we are strong and solid as well as open and intimate, that we have backbone <u>and</u> heart, and that's a difficult balance for most men to achieve. Most of us are still searching for the right balance, and Men's Groups can play an important role in helping men find that balance.

Thirdly, resistance to Men's Groups may be because of the stigma associated with what Men's Groups are and a misunderstanding around how they work. Put aside images of beating your chest whilst dancing around a fire howling to the moon. Not that there's anything wrong with that, but picture instead a group of men sitting around a circle, sharing their challenges freely, giving and receiving feedback and support. It's as simple and as powerful as that.

We need to redefine what Men's Groups are, dispel the myths, and move beyond the misconceptions and judgments.

Being a solid man, a dependable husband and a present father can be really challenging. I am so clear that the man I am for my wife and the father I am to my four children is inextricably bound to the growth and development I have experienced from being in a Men's Group.

Men's Groups provide an opportunity for men to become better communicators. They are a safe space to be open, authentic and vulnerable and to understand and manage our emotions. Men's Groups are a vehicle for men to be honest with others and with ourselves, to support each other with our struggles and to share our triumphs. They're about calling each other on our bullshit, holding each other accountable and helping each other to gain clarity in all aspects of a man's life.

This is what men need, and it's also what women want for the men in their lives.

Ultimately, Men's Groups are about challenging each other to confront and embrace the realities, the responsibilities, and the opportunities of being a man, a husband, and a father. I am eternally grateful to the men in my Men's Group for their role in the man I am today, and I know my family, friends and work colleagues will reap the rewards for many years to come.

For this is the journey that men make to find themselves.

If they fail in this, it doesn't matter much what else they find.

Money, position, fame, many loves, revenge are all of little consequence and when the tickets are collected at the end of the ride, they are tossed into the bin marked failure.

But, if a man happens to find himself—if he knows what he can be depended upon to do, the limits of his courage, the positions from which he will no longer retreat, the degree to which he can surrender his inner life to some woman, the secret reservoirs of his determination, the extent of his dedication, the depth of his feelings for beauty, his honest and unpostured goals—then he has found a mansion which he can inhabit with dignity all the days of his life.

James Michener

Chapter 8
Why Join A Men's Group?

"Everyone (even terrorists and killers) are doing the best they can right now due to the parenting, upbringing, learning, life experiences, culture, level of consciousness, past programming, etc. that have made them who they are. Just as you want to be accepted for who you are and you have all the stuff you did in your life you are not proud of. That is all you could do at that time. Therefore, learn to forgive yourself and your enemies and those you judge. They could not have been different from who they were at that time. Therefore, do not take life personally. It is none of your business what others think of you. We are each on our own inner journey. Accept them as you want them to accept you."

John Robson (www.higherawareness.com)

This is the primary reason to join a men's group: To join a group of men who recognize that we all make mistakes and have done things that we aren't necessarily proud of, though that does not necessarily mean that we are bad men; to create an environment in which a man feels safe enough to share his deepest secrets and pain and his greatest joys; a place where men can get "real" about their inner world of thoughts, feelings and beliefs and share them without fear of judgment, attack or ridicule; a place in which all men are held accountable for their words and actions and are willing to stay in integrity with their deepest truths.

Within a men's group, men bring awareness to their unconscious beliefs about what it means to be a man and they uncover any erroneous beliefs they may have about themselves that may be keeping them from being genuinely happy with their lives.

The truth is we always make the best possible choice for ourselves in that moment based on our limited amount of understanding. In other words, if we knew better, we'd do better. Of course, we must always be willing to accept the consequences of our choices, so if we aren't happy with our consequences we must first change our awareness and understanding so that we can make better ones. So the key to making better choices is to expand your understanding. Men's work is designed to help you do that.

With that being said, is it really possible for a man to create and maintain a rewarding and fulfilling life? Actually, is it possible for a man to create an extraordinary life? In order to answer this question, you must first decide what extraordinary means to you. So how would you define extraordinary?

For me, an extraordinary life is a life in which a man is truly happy with all aspects of his life. First and foremost, he is happy with himself. He has taken the time to fully understand who he is and what makes him tick. He has taken the road less traveled and made a conscious decision to uncover all the emotional and psychological barriers that would keep him from expressing who he really is. He has done his "inner work" and exercised all of his inner demons and has shined a light on the dark places within his soul. Through a process of self-reflection and introspection, he has become aware that he is perfect as a result of his imperfections and he has learned to accept himself just the way he is. He recognizes that self-love is the key to his happiness and he makes this his top priority in life.

Once he has learned to truly love himself, he then makes a conscious effort to develop and maintain intimate, authentic and connected relationships. He recognizes that relationships are the glue that holds his life together and he insures that all of his relationships are deep and satisfying. He no longer has drama and stress in relationships because he understands that all relationships begin within him and once he has created an inner self-love relationship with himself, he is then able to create that type of relationship with another. He understands that life is meant to be shared, and he chooses to find the right partner to share life with and he never takes that relationship for granted. He nurtures it daily and makes a conscious effort to continually deepen it by being emotionally and psychologically present within his environment of love.

He makes his personal relationships a very high priority in his life and he is rewarded with relationships and friendships that truly nurture and sustain him. In his family life, he develops deep family connections with his partner and children and he insures that his family always comes first before external relationships. His family is his greatest joy and he relishes the responsibility of being a great husband/partner and father.

In his professional life, he recognizes the importance of integrity and honesty in all of his interactions and he holds himself accountable for being authentic and real in all of his interactions. He shies away from judgment and gossip and always looks for the best in his associates and co-workers.

Next on the list is dynamic health. He recognizes the beauty and complexity of the human body and he maintains a deep reverence for this amazing miracle. He understands the importance of taking care of his physical body by eating healthy food, maintaining a healthy weight and by exercising the body to keep it operating at its maximum capacity. He is consciously aware that without his health he can never fully enjoy his life.

To insure that his life is rewarding and fulfilling, he chooses a vocation that nurtures his soul. He refuses to work at a job that he hates and he recognizes that if he isn't happy with his work it is his responsibility to find work that he enjoys. Although making money is important, he recognizes that he should not lose his soul in the pursuit of wealth. At the same time he must be financially responsible with his money and not fall victim to materialism and consumerism. He commits to earning a sufficient amount of money to do what he loves and he makes smart decisions that will allow him to save money for a rainy day and ride off into the sunset in his retirement years with adequate financial resources.

Last, but definitely not least, he develops an intimate connection with a power greater than himself. He does not have to accept or adhere to any organized religion filled with dogma or doctrine. He simply makes a conscious choice to accept that he has access to a divine intelligence that permeates all things and flows through him at all times. He is

Chapter 8 ~ Why Join A Men's Group?

aware and connected to this intelligence and he develops a practice that deepens this connection and nurtures his spirit. By embracing this philosophy, he learns that all things are intimately connected and this gives him a deep sense of reverence and awe for this amazing gift called life.

So I'll ask the question again. Is it possible for a man to live an extraordinary life? Can a man create everything that I just mentioned? Can he create inner peace, great relationships, dynamic health, rewarding careers and a spiritual connection that nurtures his soul? I believe the answer is yes and a great place to start would be by joining a men's group.

There is a good chance that the thought of meeting with a group of men to talk about your feelings might cause you to feel uncomfortable. This is normal. The reason you may be feeling uncomfortable is because you may be trapped in the antiquated paradigm of masculinity that I keep talking about. Why do you think it's so difficult for men to do this? Because from a very young age, in boyhood, we are taught and conditioned to believe that men shouldn't feel. We are taught that feelings are for women and for wimps and sissies, right? Wrong! Feelings are the language of our soul and if we are unable to feel and express them we miss out on the most important aspect of life, which is intimacy and connection. We cannot experience intimacy and connection without our emotions so it's important for us to learn how to feel if we truly want our connections and relationships to be real.

As I mentioned earlier in this book, after my divorce back in 1989, I spiraled into a deep state of depression. I felt like an absolute failure.

I was confused, depressed and filled with a deep sense of internalized shame about myself. I isolated myself for months until the pain became so unbearable that I reached a point where I only had two choices. Get help, or die. Fortunately for me, I chose to live and I gathered the courage to get help.

Unfortunately, too many men are currently at a point in their lives where they feel the same way. Their lives are spiraling out of control and they have no idea what to do next. If you're reading this book, chances are you may be in that situation right now. If you are, there is a good chance that you have isolated yourself from others and may not have a support system to support you during challenging times. Since most men are uncomfortable sharing their feelings openly, they refuse to say the three most difficult words for a man to say; "I NEED HELP". It takes courage and vulnerability to say these words and most men do not even have the emotional vocabulary or awareness to utter them. But until a man fully understands the importance of seeking support he can never change.

Herein lies the reason for a man to join a men's group. Within the context of the group, men learn that it is okay to say I need help. As a matter of fact, they learn that there is actually strength in saying so. In a men's group, men create an environment in which they can speak openly and honestly about anything. Men create a container in which they know that no matter what they share they will not be judged, attacked or criticized and will be listened to with compassion and empathy. It is within this context that men can heal. When a group of men come together to discuss how they really feel, what they really think and what they truly believe about themselves, it opens the door to transformation.

Chapter 8 ~ Why Join A Men's Group?

This is no easy task. The current culture of masculinity actually discourages men from having these types of interactions and conversations. Our culture encourages us to talk about things like sports, sex, politics, religion and making money but it doesn't encourage us to talk about our hurts, fears, dreams, ambitions and joys. These are "inner" conversations that deal with the heart and very few men can communicate from their hearts. The power of men's groups is that it supports men in taking the longest journey of their lives—the eighteen-inch journey from their heads to their hearts.

Once a man takes this journey, it changes everything. He awakens to the depth and beauty of being a man and he embraces the truth that he is perfect as a result of his imperfections. He embraces his strengths and weaknesses, his darkness and his light. He learns how to accept himself for the man he is and he realizes that the only competition he has is with himself. He commits to becoming the best man that he can be and he learns that self love is the armor that protects him from any external criticism or attack. By wearing this armor, he creates a world of love and understanding by loving himself and understanding others.

Join a men's group today!

"It's hard to get people to overcome the thought that they have to take care of themselves first. It's hard to get players to give in to the group and become selfless as opposed to selfish."

Isaiah Thomas

Chapter 9
Starting A Men's Group

Hopefully this book has provided you with enough insights to encourage you to consider joining a men's group. I'm sure there are still lots of questions you may have and one of the most important ones might be how to find a men's group to join. The good news is there are endless resources now available for men when it comes to men's work. I've included a list of them in the final chapter of this book. You must simply decide that you want to join one and then find one and get started.

There are two types of groups you can consider. First, there are live meetings in which men get together on a regular basis. To join this type of group, you will obviously be limited to groups within your geographical area. I believe live groups offer the greatest opportunity for growth. Nothing compares to sitting in a group of committed men who are there for you physically, emotionally and spiritually. Being able to develop intimate connections and friendships with other men is priceless. Having access to friends that you can physically interact with and share your heart and truth with is invaluable.

Next, there are virtual groups. These are online groups using video conferencing technology that allow men to get together by video from anywhere in the world and create a community environment. Rest assured that virtual meetings are powerful and effective. The key is to find a group of committed men who are willing to commit to their own growth and the growth of the group. As long as the men are committed to being open, vulnerable and real, I can assure you that virtual groups can help facilitate growth and transformation. Men can bond and connect through a virtual environment in the same way that men in a live environment can.

No matter which type of group you choose, the key to your success lies in your willingness to get started and fully participate. You must decide that you are 100% committed to learning and growing and you cannot let anything stand in the way of your growth.

If you can't find a group in your area or online, you might consider starting your own group. This may seem a bit overwhelming and difficult but rest assured you can do it if you're serious enough about your own growth. As mentioned, there are an unlimited amount of resources available to you if you truly want to be in a group. Do not let your fear keep you from joining or starting a group.

If you're considering starting a group of your own, I would like to share some keys to starting a men's group. These keys come from an organization co-founded by a friend of mine named Tom Daly. His organization is called The Men's Leadership Alliance and it is a wonderful organization that focuses on developing programs for men.

Be sure to check out their website and sign up for their newsletter. They offer wonderful programs for men.

Be sure to read through this article they wrote about starting and running a men's group. It provides a great framework for starting and maintaining a successful men's group.

Starting & Running a Successful Men's Group

www.mensleadershipalliance.org

Here's a list of basic principles that have proven useful in starting and running men's groups. We offer them as an invitation to discover your own guidelines and not as rigid rules of order.

Men's groups have from 5 to 12 members and are usually closed to new members after the formation stage. Our community also sponsors **open groups** twice a month so that men who are new to the work can explore the possibility of creating or join an established group. The focus is on authenticity, connection, mutual support and personal soul work.

Take the risk and do it.

If you want to be in a men's group and there are none in your area then you must take the risk and put out a call. This can take any form that works for you: flyers in public gathering places, therapist's offices, or restaurants, etc. or you can start a Facebook page or simply call and email potential participants. You can start a group with just yourself and one other man then each find another man, and those men find 4 other men and that makes the group of 8. There is awesome power in intention.

Get commitment to the group.

Getting commitment to the group is essential. Spend whatever time it takes to get some agreement about what group members are committing to, both in terms of intentions and time. We recommend that several sessions early on be devoted to giving each man ample opportunity to make his needs and intentions known. Most groups ask for a certain time commitment to build the container. Three to six months gives most groups time to know if things will work. It is a good idea to meet every two weeks, but some groups meet every week and some meet monthly. Just decide what works for your group and stick to it.

Expect everyone to show up for every scheduled meeting and notify the others when they can't make it. If you don't make the group a priority in your life, it won't be. All members should be committed. If someone decides to leave the group they should notify the group and have some sort of closer. Even when only one man leaves, the group chemistry changes and you need to ritualize the ending of the old and the beginning of a new group.

Respect confidentiality.

A strong group depends upon the willingness of the members to keep it strong. The most important part of that strength is confidentiality. It is also important to recognize that the men will talk about what happens at meetings to someone, sometime, so it's a good idea to know where everyone's boundaries are on this issue. It is good to make clear with your group that if men speak to others about what happened at a meeting you do so <u>very</u> selectively and in the same spirit in which it was spoken (in a sacred context). Men should speak only from their own personal perspective and avoid discussing and speaking about another men's experience. Men should agree to get permission to make <u>anything</u> public.

Mark a gateway in space and time.

We believe group time is very special and out of the ordinary. Consciously recognizing the particular time and space of the meeting gives us more power to work with. We usually move some furniture around so that we have an open area in the center, light a candle and put it in the center. We have also used cloth, rocks, sticks, knives, pipes and other items as part of our centerpiece.

Formal openings can start by sitting quietly for several minutes with your eyes closed. Internally, each man centers himself in his own way. Then open your eyes and make contact with each man there. Often one member will smudge the group with sage or make an evocation for the evening calling the seven directions.

Sit in a circle at the same eye level.

It is important that all members are in this as equals, and sitting at the same eye level makes that a concrete reality. For some groups this is more important than others. Just see how it feels for your group.

Share leadership and take "radical freedom".

Agree that everyone in the group is responsible for the course of events at all times, even when one man is serving in the role of leader for the evening. Taking "radical freedom" means being honest and strong enough not to go along with any process that doesn't feel right. You can either sit out and witness, or, if the feeling is strong enough and you sense that something is "off", you can call for a check-in time. We view this way of operating as our highest priority. We want group work to cut through the old patterns of suppressing our inner knowings. If some members are new or have difficulty speaking up, it may be necessary to build in checkpoints. The more everyone feels responsible and respected for his input, the more vital the group will be.

Using a talking object.

The talking object is a stone, feather, staff or any object we choose that signifies who the speaker will be. With it we ensure that each man will get his say without interruption. Our guidelines for its use are: speak your own truth, speak from personal experience, speak and listen from your heart, no interruptions while another is speaking, each man has an opportunity to speak before anyone speaks a second time (even if it's to say that he passes), let feelings be, don't rescue one another, end when it feels like everyone has had their say, and last but not least, keep it brief and to the point. We often have a time-keeper who lets each man know when he has spoken for the agreed upon time limit.

Speak your truth. Be willing to face conflict and shadow.

This has to be the toughest guideline to follow and is perhaps our greatest gift to one another. This especially includes negative judgments and feelings one group member has toward another. Everyone is responsible for expressing conflicts openly and directly. We have found that it helps to make "I" statements but that rule sometimes gets tossed out in the heat of the moment. So we have to be willing to apologize and admit mistakes when we go over the line into shame or blame.

As men, we are trained to draw away from another man's uncomfortable truths and pain, to avoid vulnerable or embarrassing feelings that might come up, or to use the discomfort to our advantage when dealing with a competitor. Only by staying present and being courageous can we continue to draw our attention to what is really going on. We all agree to hang in there when the going gets tough and to support one another through these difficult times. Fortunately, this guideline gets easier over time as we learn to trust the process. No group will last without being able to handle conflict. When one man as an issue with another, it is important to have a process in place to handle it. (See the **Conflict Facilitation Model** we use as an example.)

We also remind one another that all personal business has a larger social, political and spiritual component. How each of us is doing his own work affects the whole group and the larger communities of which we are all a part. Our groups provide support and training for our work in the world.

Use ritual to access the many realms.

Ritual is the bridge between the physical, psychological, the socio-political, the mythic and the causal realms. We define the sacred space with a simple ritual opening and closing, and we use ritual within that space to give multi-dimensionality to our words, feelings, dreams and visions.

We apply the principle of radical freedom with special diligence in all our ritual work. Ritual without freedom is oppressive and opposed to what we are striving for. Men's groups are containers for soul work. We are constantly opening to deeper and deeper levels of ourselves, our brothers, and to the mysteries of life.

Share leadership.

When groups first begin, it is often appropriate for one or two men with more experience to lead the group and provide structure. The ideal after a few months is to share leadership among all members of the group on a rotating basis. Even on a given evening, responsibilities can be shared. If your groups use the 4 archetype model of King, Warrior, Magician, and Lover, roles for the evening can be divided along those lines.

Open groups in our community are seen as entry points, practice for developing group skills, and since the composition of these groups changes from month to month, all open groups are facilitated by an experienced leader.

Look for changes in your group members and yourself.

If we expect the group members to stay the same, the group energy will wane. One of our greatest gifts to one another is that we can often see changes in others that they haven't yet noticed in themselves. We can see them in their fullness and beauty, and we can encourage and honor their development. We all grow strong in the blessing, support and appreciation of one another.

Make group business a higher priority than worldly business.

In our meetings, personal business and soul work are the first priority. Outside business is discussed in the context of how it impacts us personally. We avoid working with the details and logistics of any outside activity until personal business has been taken care of first.

Make a clear closing.

It is important to mark the end of your meeting in some way. You can join hands and remain silent for a few minutes. Or each man can give thanks in his own way and makes a closing statement. Or men can make eye contact and release the circle by blowing out the candle. Find a way that works for your group. This is important.

Honor free social time.

We usually save personal conversations for before or after the meeting, but we are very aware of the need for and importance of open time. In most successful groups, some of the members have contact with one another outside lodge meetings. Occasionally we schedule meals or other events where interactions can flow more spontaneously.

A basic model for group structure:

- All men greet one another.
- (Prior to the meeting, decide on leadership responsibilities.)
- Secure the privacy of the space.
- Gather in a circle.
- Welcome each man into the circle.

- Light a candle in the center of the circle, sit quietly for a few minutes or call the 7 directions. (Sage smoke is often used in our circles.)

- Confirm confidentiality and guidelines for the group.

- First level check in. Short and to the point about how each man's life is going.

- Second level check-in. Share what is going on at the soul level. We often ask how burning the issue is and if the man would like some support.

- Check to be sure no man has a conflict with another man in the group. If so, clear that conflict using the model below.

- If no man is in need of special attention and there are no conflicts, the group leader can offer a process the whole group can share in.

- Either paired or whole group sharing about the process.

- Appreciations and blessing circle round.

- Announcements.

- Final check out. Ending with eye contact and releasing the circle. (Blow out the candle, release the 7 directions, or a final collective breath.)

Until one is committed, there is hesitancy, the chance to draw back, always ineffectiveness. Concerning all acts of initiative (and creation), there is one elementary truth, the ignorance of which kills countless ideas and splendid plans: that the moment one definitely commits oneself, then Providence moves too. All sorts of things occur to help one that would never otherwise have occurred. A whole stream of events issues from the decision, raising in one's favor all manner of unforeseen incidents and meetings and material assistance, which no man could have dreamt would have come his way. I have learned a deep respect for one of Goethe's couplets:

Whatever you can do, or dream you can, begin it.

Boldness has genius, power, and magic in it!

William Hutchison Murray

Chapter 10
Resources

Commitment can be defined as "an internal promise that we make to ourselves that we won't quit." Without commitment it is difficult, if not impossible, to truly transform your life. In order to live an extraordinary life, a man must make the commitment to himself that he is willing to do whatever it takes to transform himself from the inside out. This is no easy task but rest assured, if you're reading this book, you already have everything you need to do so.

As the previous quote stated: "the moment one definitely commits oneself, then Providence moves too. All sorts of things occur to help one that would never otherwise have occurred. A whole stream of events issues from the decision, raising in one's favor all manner of unforeseen incidents and meetings and material assistance, which no man could have dreamt would have come his way."

During the darkest period of my life, I made the most powerful commitment that I have ever made to myself. I made the commitment that I would figure out how to become genuinely happy with my life.

At the time, I had absolutely no idea how I was going to do this but I intuitively knew I would, somehow. I had no money, no friends, no job, no relationship and no clue what steps I needed to take to become happy but I simply made the commitment that no matter what it took and no matter how long it would take I was going to be happy with my life.

As soon as I made the commitment, miracles began to happen. All of a sudden, a series of synchronistic events began to occur and I learned to trust my own inner wisdom to guide me. Another word for inner wisdom is intuition and as soon as I learned to listen to it and trust it, my life made a huge turn for the better.

My intuition became the guiding force in my life and, without question, it guided me to the perfect people, events and experiences I needed to put my life back together and to now be able to say that I'm happier than I've ever been in my life.

In our current culture, we have been conditioned to believe that only women have intuition but I can assure you that nothing could be further from the truth. Men are just as intuitive as women and when we commit to listening to and trusting our intuition it can guide us along our journey of healing and transformation.

Now that you've arrived at the end of this book, it's up to you to listen to your own inner wisdom and intuition. Rest assured that you have access to it but you must commit to connecting to it. If you accept the ideas in this book and are willing to follow its guidance, I'm certain that your intuition will guide you to the next step you need to take along your journey of transformation.

As I mentioned before, I have come to believe that the three most difficult words for a man to say are, I need help! These three simple words hold the key to your growth and transformation. Until you are able to utter these words to yourself and then share them with others, you will never change. I hope you've learned that it's okay to seek support as you've read through this book. So heed my advice and simply begin by recognizing that no man is an island and he must be willing to acknowledge his connectedness to others. Begin by acknowledging that you cannot go on this journey alone and allow yourself to be supported and encouraged along the way. Your journey may begin with a book (which is why you're reading this one), a coaching session, a trip to a therapist, a workshop or seminar or even some quiet time in silence and self-introspection. It doesn't matter how you start, simply start. And remember the wise words of Dr. Martin Luther King, "You don't have to see the whole staircase to take the first step." Take the step and begin your journey.

With that being said, I would like to offer a list of resources that I am absolutely certain can empower and support you on your journey. Each of these resources is committed to empowering men to embrace the new paradigm of masculinity that I've been speaking about throughout this book so you are in good hands with each of them.

What you must be willing to do is find the resource that resonates with you and commit to contacting the resource for yourself. Trust your own inner wisdom as you review the attached resources and do not be afraid to reach out to any of the people on this list. Some of the resources offer courses while others provide coaching and programs that can definitely help you on your journey of transformation. Know that you're not alone and there are men from all around the globe who would love to connect with you and support you on your journey.

I want to close this book by acknowledging you for having the courage to begin your journey. I know how difficult and challenging it is to embrace some of the ideas in this book and I also know that if I can overcome all of the adversity I've shared in this book, then you too can overcome any challenge you may be facing in your own life.

So take a moment and acknowledge yourself right now for the amazing man you are. Seriously, look in the mirror right now and say this simple mantra; "Every day in every way, I keep getting better and better and I deserve the best life has to offer." Use this as an affirmation and repeat it to yourself daily and I can assure you that it will have a positive impact on your life.

You can have it all but you have to decide what "all" means to you. Whatever your definition of all may be, know that you can have it.

Never forget this powerful quote by the late Robert Schuller: "If it's to be, it's up to me!"

It's all up to you now! You got this!

Good luck!

Coach Michael Taylor

Tom Daly
www.mensleadershipalliance.org

Jayson Gaddis
www.jaysongaddis.com

Mike Hrostoski
www.theschoolformen.com

Dwayne Klassen
www.remarkablemanproject.com

Tom Kelley
www.opendeepandtrue.com

Rick Beldon
www.rickbelden.com

Christopher Sunyata
www.sunyata.info

Richard Arsic
www.richardarsic.com

Eivind Figenschau Skjellum
www.inner-throne.com

Graham Reid Phoenix
www.grahamreidphoenix.com

Enric Carbo'
www.filo.cat

Tim Fisk
www.completemen.org

Brett Churnin
www.mensgroup.info

Ayan Mukherjee
www.ayanrp.com

Mankind Project
www.mkp.org

Andrew Ferebee
www.knowledgeformen.com

Sword & Scepter Workshop
www.swordandscepter.com

Graham Stoney
www.confidentman.net

Max Warren
www.emergentmasculinity.com

Recommended Reading

King Warrior Magician Lover by Robert Moore & Douglas Gillete

Iron John by Robert Bly

Fire In The Belly by Sam Keen

A New Conversation With Men by Michael Taylor

Man Unplugged by John Broadbent

About the Author

Coach Michael Taylor is an entrepreneur, author, motivational speaker and radio show host who has dedicated his life to empowering men and women to reach their full potential. He knows firsthand how to overcome adversity and build a rewarding and fulfilling life and he is sharing his knowledge and wisdom with others to support them in creating the life of their dreams. He is no stranger to adversity and challenges. He was born in the inner city projects of Corpus Christi, Texas to a single mother with six children. Although he dropped out of high school in the 11th grade, his commitment to living an extraordinary life supported him in defying the odds.

With persistence, patience and perseverance he was able to climb the corporate ladder of success and become a very successful mid-level manager of a multi-million dollar building supply center at the tender young age of 21. After approximately eight years, he was then faced with another set of challenges as he experienced the pain and humiliation of divorce, bankruptcy and foreclosure and found himself contemplating suicide.

Bankrupt and alone, he committed to rebuilding his life which propelled him to begin a 20 year inner journey of personal transformation which resulted in him discovering his true self and his passions for living. As a result, he is now happily married (14 years) and living his dream of living an extraordinary life while being in service to others. Through his books, lectures and radio program, he now coaches others on how to become genuinely happy with their lives and live the lives they were born to live.

www.coachmichaeltaylor.com
www.adversityisyourgreatestally.com
www.creationpublishing.com
www.anewconversationwithmen.com
www.bmracademy.com

Contact us:

Email: mtaylor@ancwm.com
Phone: 877-255-3588

www.ingramcontent.com/pod-product-compliance
Lightning Source LLC
Chambersburg PA
CBHW070600300426
44113CB00010B/1331